CALIFORNIA

The Wine Country Inn, St. Helena

COUNTRY INNS OF AMERICA

California

A GUIDE TO THE INNS OF
THE NORTH COAST, MONTEREY, THE SOUTH COAST,
SAN FRANCISCO, THE WINE COUNTRY, THE GOLD COUNTRY

BY PETER ANDREWS, GEORGE ALLEN,
ROBERTA HOMAN GARDNER, AND TERRY BERGER

PHOTOGRAPHED BY GEORGE W. GARDNER,
LILO RAYMOND, AND MICHAEL REID

DESIGNED BY ROBERT REID

HOLT, RINEHART AND WINSTON, *New York*

Cover and frontispiece: Britt House, San Diego.

Back cover: City Hotel, Columbia.

Maps, Anthony St. Aubyn.
Editorial assistance, Marian Reid.

Photographs on the following pages are used with permission from The Knapp Press, 5900 Wilshire Blvd, Los Angeles, CA 90036, © 1978 and 1980 by Knapp Communications Corporation: 1, 16–20, 22–25, 30–35, 38–47, 54–56, 58–61, 64, 65, 68–73, 78–81, 88–91, 97–102, 104, 105, 124, 125, 130–133, 137–141, 150–155, 162–169, 178–183, 188–190, 192.

Published by Holt, Rinehart and Winston, 383 Madison Avenue, New York, New York 10017.
Published simultaneously in Canada by Holt, Rinehart and Winston of Canada, Limited.

Library of Congress Cataloging in Publication Data
Main entry under title:
California, a guide to the inns of the North Coast,
    Monterey, the South Coast, San Francisco, the Wine
    Country, the Gold Country.
    (Country inns of America)
    Rev. ed. of: California, a guide to the inns of
California / by Peter Andrews and George Allen. 1st ed.
1980.

    1. Hotels, taverns, etc.—California—Directories.
I. Andrews, Peter, 1931– . Calfornia, a guide to the
inns of California. II. Series.
TX907.C28   1983   647′.9479401   83-7059

ISBN Hardbound: 0-03-062756-7
ISBN Paperback: 0-03-068681-4

First Edition

10 9 8 7 6 5 4 3 2 1

A Robert Reid production

Printed in Hong Kong

ISBN 0-03-062756-7 HARDBOUND
ISBN 0-03-068681-4 PAPERBACK

THE INNS

All photographs by
George W. Gardner,
except as credited.

*Photographed by
Lilo Raymond.

**Photographed by
Michael Reid.

NORTH COAST
MONTEREY
SOUTH COAST

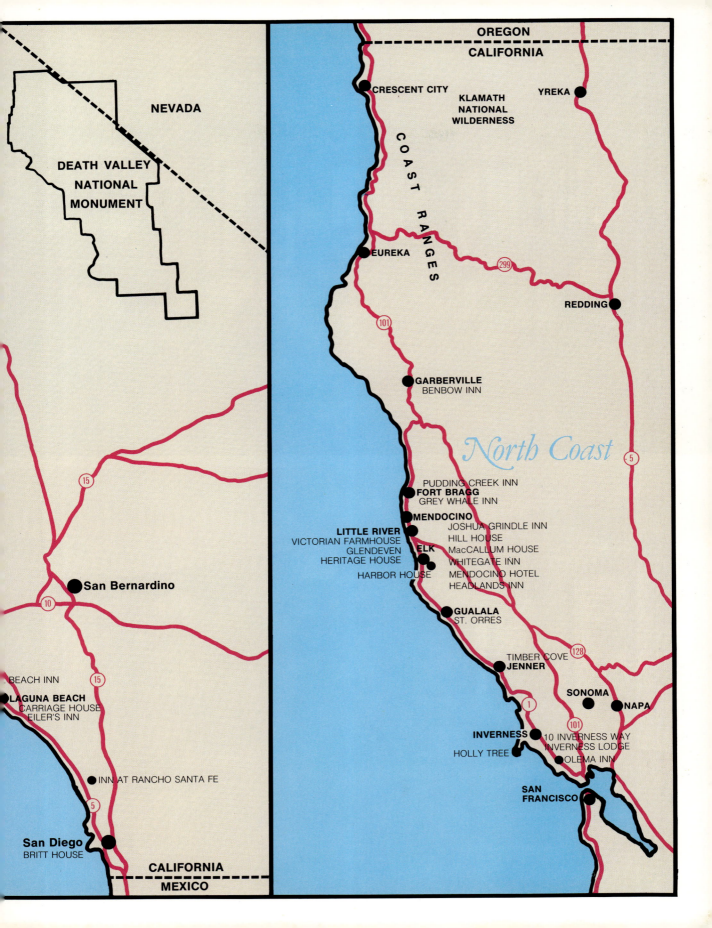

NEVADA

DEATH VALLEY NATIONAL MONUMENT

OREGON
CALIFORNIA

CRESCENT CITY

KLAMATH NATIONAL WILDERNESS

YREKA

C O A S T   R A N G E S

EUREKA

299

REDDING

101

GARBERVILLE
Benbow Inn

North Coast

5

PUDDING CREEK INN
FORT BRAGG
GREY WHALE INN
MENDOCINO
JOSHUA GRINDLE INN
LITTLE RIVER   HILL HOUSE
VICTORIAN FARMHOUSE   MacCALLUM HOUSE
GLENDEVEN   **ELK**
HERITAGE HOUSE   WHITEGATE INN
                     MENDOCINO HOTEL
HARBOR HOUSE   HEADLANDS INN

GUALALA
ST. ORRES

128

TIMBER COVE
JENNER

SONOMA

1   **NAPA**

101

INVERNESS 10 INVERNESS WAY
               INVERNESS LODGE
HOLLY TREE   OLEMA INN

SAN FRANCISCO

15

San Bernardino

10

.BEACH INN   15

LAGUNA BEACH
CARRIAGE HOUSE
EILER'S INN

INN AT RANCHO SANTA FE

5

San Diego
BRITT HOUSE

CALIFORNIA
MEXICO

Innkeepers' magic transforms the Benbow

The guest rooms now have more individuality.

From Highway 101 the Benbow Inn is an imposing sight, its sturdy Tudor beams complementing the drama of northern California's majestic mountains. But the real magic begins inside, for innkeepers Patsy and Chuck Watts are in the process of taking this inn from the merely spectacular to the sublime.

When they bought the Benbow in 1978, the Watts were no strangers to the inn business, having spent several years in Carmel creating the Vagabond House Inn. The gracious old Benbow, which first opened its doors in 1926, offered an enormous challenge, for its stately mien had begun to fall into disrepair. Through tireless effort, the inn is being completely restored and graced with their superb sense of style.

The lobby alone is a Renaissance dream. Ancestral portraits, bronze, ivory, and wooden statuary, framed needlepoint, wonderful clocks and books, and richly upholstered settees define the pillared alcoves which flank the room. A carved walnut fireplace, abundant fresh flowers and greenery, and Muffin, a languid Afghan hound, add great warmth and appeal. In fact, it's difficult to leave this wonderful space. But moving on, you discover the Fox and Horn, with its leather easy chairs, roaring fire, and jukebox filled with big band favorites, and the Hunt Room, in which a classic movie is shown each night.

The Benbow is also blessed with an extremely adept chef whose skills may be enjoyed in the formal dining room, overlooking the rushing waters of the Eel River which flows past at the foot of the lawn. Specialties of the house include roast duck in apricot and grand marnier sauce, milk-fed veal sautéed with lemon, white wine and capers, and breast of chicken stuffed with fruits and nuts and lapped with a delicate curry sauce. The house dessert, a chocolate mousse pie, is a concoction so rich and subtle that its recipe is a guarded secret.

Guest rooms, all aglow in shades of deep rose and soft yellow, are comfortably furnished with a blend of antiques and reproductions and each is provided with a basket filled with paperback mysteries for a quick and relaxing read.

The Watts took care that the Benbow's outdoor pleasures match its interior delights by planting a formal English rose garden and a veritable forest of Japanese maples which insure vibrant fall color. And, as luck would have it, each summer the park service dams the river to form a lake. The inn is a fortunate neighbor to this annual project and installs a sand beach, to the delight of guests.

Left: The richly furnished lobby is reminiscent of an English country house, with exotic Watts' touches. OVERLEAF: The inn sits majestically in the gentle, green countryside of northern California.

BENBOW INN, 2675 Benbow Dr., Garberville, CA 95440; (707) 923-2124; Patsy and Chuck Watts, Innkeepers. A large, sumptuous inn, built in 1920s Tudor style, in the heart of California's redwood country. The 54 guest rooms include 4 deluxe units. All private baths. Open April 1 to Dec. 1. Reopens for holidays Dec. 16 to Jan. 2. Rates: double, $65 to $150 range. Breakfast, a buffet lunch and a lavish dinner are served daily. In good weather, meals are served on the terrace. A Champagne brunch is served on Sunday. During fall and winter, tea and biscuits are served afternoons in the lobby. Live piano music nightly in the cocktail lounge. Children not encouraged. No pets. No cigar smoking anywhere in the inn. All major credit cards accepted. A "Nutcracker Christmas" and New Year's celebration, December 18 to January 2. Beach for sunbathing, swimming in a private lake, and a 9-hole golf course. Canoeing and hiking in the redwood forest are other popular activities.

DIRECTIONS: From San Francisco, follow US 101 approximately 200 miles north to Benbow exit. Inn is on left-hand side of US 101.

PUDDING CREEK INN

Fort Bragg   **NORTH COAST**

Genuine country charm

The Pudding Creek Inn was built in 1884 by a Russian expatriate count known to Fort Bragg locals as "Bottle Brown." The story goes that the count absconded from his country with enough illegal funds to enable him to build a small empire in Fort Bragg, including these two Victorian houses on Main Street. The inn is owned by Marilyn and Gene Gunderson, who are gradually uncovering the building's original charm and historic artifacts. The countess's wedding gown, the exact picture of which Marilyn has found in the first Montgomery Ward catalogue, is on display in the storefront gift shop, as are depression glass, old fashioned candies, and local handcrafts. Rooms upstairs and in the inn's adjoining house are decorated simply but with such homey touches as a spinning wheel or a child's school desk. The special treasures at the Pudding Creek are Marilyn's homemade breakfast breads, which come from midwestern recipes out of her Indiana past. These celestial morsels are served daily in the inn's country kitchen or in the greenhouse which connects the two houses.

This guest room is not typical, but illustrates the thought that has gone into the inn.

PUDDING CREEK INN, 700 N. Main St., Fort Bragg, CA 95437; (707) 964-9529; Marilyn and Gene Gunderson, Innkeepers. The inn, two Victorian houses connected by a garden court, has 11 guest rooms, all with private bath. Open all year. Rates: $35 to $55 double, including Continental breakfast. No other meals served; there are a number of restaurants in the area. Complementary wine on arrival. Children over 10 years welcome. No pets. Visa, MasterCard accepted. An antique and gift shop on the premises offers interesting shopping. Beaches, tennis courts and bicycle paths nearby. Ride the California Western Railroad (The Skunk) from Fort Bragg to Willits. Daily trips year round and special shorter excursions in summer. Station 2½ blocks away.
   DIRECTIONS: From San Francisco US 101 north to either Rte. 128 or Rte. 20 to Rte. 1, which becomes Main street in Fort Bragg.

Fort Bragg | # GREY WHALE INN | **NORTH COAST**

Whale-viewing is optional

Grey whales can be watched from this inn during the months of December through April, as they migrate from the Arctic to Baja, California, and back again. Swimming one-quarter to one-half mile off shore, pods of whales go by, bringing back the young they gave birth to in southern California.

The Grey Whale Inn is located in the town of Fort Bragg, a lumber mill town. A treat awaits you! Fort Bragg is headquarters for Georgia Pacific's Skunk train. In addition to its regular run—taking lumber out and bringing supplies to the mills—there is a passenger service to Willits. Open observation cars allow passengers to enjoy to the fullest the thrill of being in the heart of the redwoods.

Prior to 1975, The Grey Whale Inn was the community's hospital. The operating room is now a guest room, and the delivery room has an ocean view. The nursery next door is a pleasant breakfast room. Its likeable owners, John and Colette Bailey, use the head doctor's office and examining room as part of their private quarters.

Because it was built as a hospital, the inn offers a bonus for handicapped guests. There is a ramp entrance at the rear and a bathroom set up to accommodate a wheelchair.

THE GREY WHALE INN, 615 N. Main St., Fort Bragg, CA 95437; (707) 964-0640; John and Collette Bailey, Innkeepers. Inn has 14 spacious guest rooms, 12 with private baths, 2 penthouse rooms share; 1 bath equipped for wheelchair. Double, queen, and king-size beds; 1 fireplace; 4 rooms with kitchens; some ocean views. Open all year. Rates: $30 to $45 single, $35 to $50 double, additional person $12. Includes Continental breakfast. No other meals served. Children welcome. No pets. Visa, MasterCard, American Express accepted. Games and books available in the parlor. July 4th world's largest Salmon Barbeque. Labor Day weekend, Paul Bunyan celebration.

DIRECTIONS: Ten miles north of Mendocino on Rte. 1, which becomes Main Street. From the north leave US 101 at Leggett or Willits for a winding scenic drive through the redwoods to Fort Bragg.

PHOTO: FRAN D. MILISTER

A unique inn building of weathered redwood.

JOSHUA GRINDLE INN

Mendocino

NORTH COAST

Resonates with echoes from earlier days

Gwen and Bill Jacobson have long been charmed by the simple comforts and lean sensibility of New England. When they learned that Joshua Grindle's home, which Grindle built in 1879 after moving to Mendocino from Maine, was for sale they knew it was for them. Deleting extraneous Victorian embellishments, they completely renovated the house, adding a private bath to each room and furnishing it with their extensive collection of seventeenth- and eighteenth-century American antiques.

The focal point of the dining room is a ten-and-one-half-foot harvest table, circa 1830, on which is served the morning repast of homemade bread or hot muffins, fresh fruit, a boiled egg, and a choice of hot breakfast brews. A fine old china cabinet and antique clock enhance the simple setting. Guest rooms maintain the pared-down feeling of New England with a few select accessories blending with brass or four-poster beds and handmade quilts.

Left: Aesop's fables are depicted in the Minton tiles that surround the hearth in one of the guest rooms.

In the evening, guests may retire to the drawing room for a tot of sherry to be sipped in front of the blazing hearth. Pianists might try their hand at the baby-grand piano or challenge a partner to a round of backgammon or chess at the corner game table. If that sounds too strenuous, you might just sit and ponder the days when Mendocino was populated by a sturdy breed of New Englanders, people who moved across the continent to find their fortune in timber and in the sea. The Joshua Grindle Inn truly resonates with echoes from those days.

JOSHUA GRINDLE INN, 44800 Little Lake, P.O. Box 647, Mendocino, CA 95460; (707) 937-4143; Bill and Gwen Jacobson, Innkeepers. This white Victorian house with fine views of the village, bay, and ocean was built by Joshua Grindle in 1879. The inn has 5 light and airy guest rooms. Private baths. Rates: $53 to $65 double, includes a full breakfast, with homemade breads and jellies. Some of the rooms have ocean views; 2 have fireplaces. Two rooms in a New England-style cottage have queen-size beds and Franklin stoves. The Jacobsons' collection of antiques is found throughout the house. No restaurant. Children limited. No pets. Eight weeks advance notice for weekends. Open all year. No credit cards accepted.

DIRECTIONS: Take Rte. 1 to Mendocino. From south, second turn-off is Little Lake. From north, first turn-off is Little Lake.

One of the Jacobson's rarest collectibles is a 1947 Pontiac station wagon.

Up-to-date Victorian on the North Coast

The idea that Victorians and the houses they lived in were somehow quaint is a modern misreading of that extraordinary period of history. The Victorians, quite properly, saw themselves as the most modern of people who built their homes with an eye for solid comfort and with appreciation of all the modern conveniences of the time, whether it be kitchen gadgetry, labor-saving devices or indoor plumbing.

The Hill House, set in the picturesque town of Mendocino on the northern California coast, is perfectly in keeping with its Victorian appearance. Built only last year, Hill House captures the spaciousness of Victorian architecture while providing each of the twenty-one guest rooms with its own telephone and private bath. There is also a color television set in each room, but each has been enclosed in a Victorian cabinet, discreetly hidden from those who prefer looking at the Pacific Ocean to watching reruns of

All the conveniences may be strictly up to date, but the accommodations and the service reflect the style of a century ago. Each room features either a king-size brass bed or two double beds and is furnished with a Victorian-style rocker, a large gold-framed mirror, oak tables and chairs, marble-topped end tables, hurricane lamps, and an abundance of freshly-cut flowers from the Hill House garden. The Fireplace Suite is much in demand, with its cozy seating area in front of the fire.

The Hill House has foundations in and plans completed for its own restaurant and bar, but for the moment guests are more than satisfied with a delightful Continental breakfast that includes juice, coffee, and homemade cake served on a tray and brought to their rooms.

The Hill House is situated in some of the most picturesque country on the north coast of California. State highway 1 runs along the coastline almost always within sight of the sea, and it is a drive of exceptional beauty. Another highly recommended trip in the area is aboard the *Super Skunk,* the splendid old California Western Railroad steam train that makes a two-hour serpentine run between Fort Bragg and Willits through the majestic redwood forests.

Not surprisingly, the area attracts a large number

Left: Recently built and decorated in the Mendocino style, the inn is a treasure.

Timeless garden flowers are always in style.

of tourists, too many for the relatively few really first-class accommodations in Mendocino. Hill House was constructed by Monte and Barbara Reed to meet that need. It took them six years to acquire permission from the State Coastal Commission to build their country inn, but when they were finished, they had created what would be unusual anywhere but in California—an instant classic.

HILL HOUSE OF MENDOCINO, 10701 Palette Dr., Mendocino, CA 95460; (707) 937-0554; Monte and Barbara Reed, Owners. Bob and Gert Permenter, Innkeepers. Although recently built, the inn was designed in perfect keeping with the architecture of this historic town, and the 21 guests rooms are furnished in Victorian decor. Private baths; phones, color TV. Rates: double and single, $56 to $95, including morning coffee and homemade coffee cake served in rooms. Each additional guest $7.50. A restaurant and bar is planned for the near future. Children welcome. No pets. No credit cards accepted. Shops and art galleries in town; many sports activities nearby.

DIRECTIONS: From San Francisco, take US 101 to Rte. 128 at Cloverdale. Turn left to Rte. 1, then north to Mendocino. Take Main St. to Lansing, turn right to Pallette Dr. and go right to inn.

The exciting Mendocino coast.

Clapboard castle, New England style

For years, when Hollywood needed a small New England town for location shooting but couldn't afford to send a crew east, they would come to Mendocino, four hours north of San Francisco. Perched on cliffs above the Pacific Ocean, Mendocino was built in the 1850s by loggers, primarily from New England and Nova Scotia, who came to work the stand of redwoods by Big River. They knew how a proper town should look—precise and practical, plain and pretty.

One of the community's gems is the MacCallum House, built in 1882 by the father of the newly-married Daisy MacCallum as a wedding present. She lived there for the next seventy-odd years, and the house is still filled with many of the original furnishings and MacCallum family memorabilia. Bill and

Sue Norris, transplanted from the East via San Francisco, bought the well-kept house in 1974 and converted it into a country inn and restaurant. It is the kind of comfortable home that brings back memories of a childhood visit to a grandmother or favorite aunt's house.

One of the few new additions to the main house is the Grey Whale Bar, beautifully built by a local carpenter from golden and California oak. The restaurant is a set of friendly rooms with dark-stained paneling and walls lined with the MacCallums' books. The menu is Continental and generally considered to be the best food in town.

The guest rooms in the main house are comfortable and cozy. One of the largest, paneled in redwood, has a sleigh bed and a view of the town. Another has white wicker furniture, a delightful contrast to the bright wallpaper. Additional accommodations have been added in the Greenhouse, snug and rustic, and the large Carriage House, with five luxurious guest rooms, a loft for the children, and a marvelous view of the cove from the living room. The Gazebo, a converted children's playhouse, is a charming miniature, but the bed is definitely large enough for grown-ups.

Distinguished pleasures of the table.

Left: A sunny porch, called the Grey Whale Bar. OVERLEAF: The inn building and a redwood-paneled guest room with a sleigh bed.

MACCALLUM HOUSE, P.O. Box 206, Mendocino, CA 95460; (707) 937-0289; Susan Norris, Innkeeper. A homey 20 room inn in a picturesque town of California's north coast. Shared baths. Open all year. Rates: $20 to $95 double, including Continental breakfast. Restaurant serves dinner daily from April to Dec. Children welcome. No pets. Visa, MasterCard accepted. Sightseeing and shopping; tennis club in town.

DIRECTIONS: From San Francisco, take US 101 to Cloverdale, exit onto Rte. 128 which leads into Rte. 1. Turn north to Mendocino 12 miles.

Where people are the most important consideration

After Wally and Robbie Clegg bought the Whitegate Inn, they recognized it on TV in *Strangers,* a Betty Davis movie. Little wonder! The inn has all the charm of a hundred year old Victorian house, plus a white picket fence, ocean view, and large cypress trees edging the north corner.

Almost always used as a residence, it began its lodging life when a middle-aged hippie artist started taking people in during the sixties. Sometimes they paid and sometimes they didn't.

The inn was partly restored by the time the Cleggs bought it in 1981 and they have refurnished and refurbished, even restoring Victorian moldings where there weren't any. All of the unique, original light fixtures are there, from hand-painted porcelain to crystal chandeliers. There is an elegant, mirrored armoire in one of the guest rooms and an old pump organ in the living room.

Breakfast is served in the dining room at a round oak table. There are banana-walnut or cinnamon-apple waffles on the weekend. The unique blend of coffee is Robbie's own, developed when she was working in a coffee shop—1/3 dark French, 1/3 light French, 1/3 Colombian. It is packaged and sold in the local cheese shop under the Whitegate Inn label.

The Cleggs offer a lot of themselves to guests. They greet them, serve wine, and recommend their own favorite restaurants. Robbie says she can feel people out when they first walk in, and knows if they want to be talked to or let alone. Being a former teacher and bartender, she's been in the people business a long time.

OVERLEAF: The town of Mendocino basks in the warm glow of the setting sun.

Left: MacCallum House, described on the previous page.

Authentically, opulently French.

WHITEGATE INN, 449 Howard St., P.O. Box 150. Mendocino, CA 95460; (707) 937-4892; Wally and Robbie Clegg, Innkeepers. This white Victorian inn offers 6 guest rooms, 3 with private baths. Each room has its own sitting area. Double, twin, and queen-size beds. Rates, including breakfast and your own decanter of wine: $45 to $65 double. In the town are many good restaurants, craft and antique shops, galleries and museums. Inn is open all year. No children. No pets. No credit cards accepted. Mendocino Headlands State Park has much to explore.

DIRECTIONS: Turn off Rte. 1 toward Mendocino business district. Howard Street is 2 blocks in.

MENDOCINO HOTEL

Where tourist and townsman meet

When Mendocino boomed as a lumber town in the last century, the headland on which it sits was crowded with houses right up to the edge of the cliffs, but time, fires, and social change have altered the town drastically. Although many of today's residents in this picturesque cluster of frame houses on California's northern coast still earn their livelihood from forest and sea, others are artists and craftsmen.

One of the principal attractions of this little headland community is the Mendocino Hotel, built in 1878, which successfully combines yesterday's architecture with today's lifestyle. Refurbished in 1973 from simple and somewhat shabby lodgings for loggers and traveling salesmen, the hotel now evokes a nostalgia for the rowdy gaudiness that characterized Mendocino in the nineteenth century when it was a rough lumberjack town. The plain, gold-colored false front is unchanged, and the interior is filled with turn-of-the-century oak, bright wallpaper, and stained and beveled glass. Upstairs, the twenty-six guest rooms have brass or carved wooden bedsteads that date from the 1880s to the 1920s and framed examples of early advertising art. Everything is keyed to comfort, and some of the accommodations have private baths. The enforced rearrangement of Mendocino's plan due to devastating fires considerably improved the hotel's view of both town and bay, and many of the rooms have balconies.

A glorious Tiffany glass dome from Philadelphia has been suspended over the carved wooden bar, a cheerful gathering place for a cross section of the town's social life. Tourists on holiday mingle easily with local artists and woodsmen, and the hotel's restaurant, which is open to the public, features local fish. Diners can choose to eat either in the dining room, with its beveled glass, oak tables and chairs, or in the Garden Room. A bright, plant-filled room off the dining room, along with the hotel's dark polished wood and oriental rugs, add to the sparkling Victorian atmosphere.

Art galleries and specialty shops in Mendocino offer good browsing, and a walk through town affords a fine prospect of the sometimes misty headlands and the weathered homes set amid flower gardens that bloom even in February.

MENDOCINO HOTEL, 45080 Main St., Mendocino, CA 95460; (707) 937-0511. A 26-room hotel, impeccably restored in the Victorian style. Private and shared baths. Open all year. Rates, including Continental breakfast: $45 to $140 double. Two guest accommodations across the bay; 1 house and 1 apartment, each housing 4 persons. Kitchens, fireplaces, and a beautiful view of the coast. Elegant dining room and two popular bars. No children under 14. No Pets. Visa, MasterCard, American Express accepted. Art galleries and specialty shops abound in this quaint New England-style village.

DIRECTIONS: From San Francisco, Mendocino is a 3½ hour drive. Take US 101 to Rte. 128, turn right onto Rte. 1. Exit onto Main St. in Mendocino. Inn is ½ mile on the right.

The light, summery lounge, *left,* contrasts with the heavier Victorian motif in the lobby, *above.*

HEADLANDS INN

Kathy cooks, Lynn gardens, Peter builds

"Travelers are treated as friends here," they say at The Headlands Inn, and they really mean it. Being friends themselves, the innkeepers value that part of innkeeping and do all they can to make their place welcoming. Kathy and Lynn met in England when they were neighbors, and Peter, a former fighter pilot and Lynn's friend, teamed up with them to buy and finish restoring the inn.

Kathy loves to cook. Loaves of bread—lemon, pumpkin, banana—appear on trays with cut flowers and the morning paper.

Lynn likes working in the garden. Daffodils, nasturtiums, daisies, and California poppies are arranged throughout the house. There are even plants in the bathrooms.

Peter, who always fancied himself a handyman, was put to the test, and succeeded! He has converted the garage into a charming cottage complete with a queen-size four-poster bed, fireplace, and oversize bathtub.

Chablis or cabernet greets guests checking in, and a comfortable common room awaits them. There are games, shelves full of books, and a card table, as well as a sleeping kitten or two.

Located in the heart of Mendocino, this elegant Victorian home enjoys an unobstructed view of the ocean. Who would suspect that it was originally a barber shop that was rolled on logs to its present location? An old Dutch proverb describes a visit to this inn: "To a friend's house the road is never long."

THE HEADLANDS INN, at Albion and Howard, P.O. Box 132, Mendocino, CA 95460; (707) 937-4431; Kathy Casper, Lynn Anderson, and Peter Albrecht, Innkeepers. The inn, a restored Victorian house, has 6 guest rooms with private baths, 4 fireplaces, 1 parlor stove, queen or king-size beds. One cottage with all amenities. Open all year. Rates, including Continental breakfast: $56 to $65 double. The town and area offer a wide choice of excellent dining places. Restaurant bookings will be made if desired. No children. No pets. No credit cards accepted. Games, books and magazines in common room. Mendocino offers many craft shops, galleries, and a variety of pleasant walks.

DIRECTIONS: Exit from Rte. 1 toward business district. Inn is at corner of Howard and Albion Streets.

For such a simple building *(left)*, the guest rooms are surprisingly distinctive *(above and overleaf)*.

Inspired collaboration of man and nature

Glendeven is a dream of ordered beauty, a place where house, lawn, and gardens have been brought together in a kind of passionate decorum. Jan deVries had known the house long before he bought it. He first visited it years ago, and he says that in some way he's tried to duplicate what he remembered of the Little River farm in every house he has owned. When he and his wife, Janet, found the original was for sale, they felt destined to buy it and take over its care.

GLENDEVEN is painted on the mailbox, and the seven-bedroom house behind the redwood fence and cypress trees might well be a private home. In its unspoiled setting on the Mendocino coast, here is an inn for calm reflection, where even the curtains at a window or the placement of a chair contribute to the sense that one is free to pursue the occupations of a bygone time.

On the main floor, a guest room looks out on the beautiful redwood-sided barn of the New England-style farm. A soft down-like comforter on the bed is a perfect covering on the cool coastal nights, and Janet has made one for every room. Upstairs, the room called King's Room has rich wine-purple walls; the Gold Crest has its own balcony; Bay View is as good as its name; Mendocino Wood has a wall of beautiful redwood paneling. At the top of the house is The Garret, where two skylights give a feeling of luxurious privacy, and muted colors are accented with a touch of chintz.

For breakfast, Janet serves muffins, coffeecakes, fruit, juices, steaming coffee, and tea in stoneware cups; and for each guest, a freshly-laid brown boiled egg comes to the table in a basket artfully made from twigs.

Outside, a rare acacia blooms in a corner of the garden, and various species of eucalyptus provide shade and exude their pungent fragrance. Pampas grass and Monterey cypresses, camellias and princess flowers all have their place. The porch gives onto a terrace edged with bright yellow flowers, and there's much for guests to see and do nearby. Down the hill is the Van Damme State Park, and two miles north the town of Mendocino spreads out along the headlands. But on most days, a pleasant stroll through the adjacent fields, with their Bishop pines, calla lilies, and flowering Scotch broom, is enough. People can easily fall in love with this part of the Pacific Coast, and Glendeven is a good place to begin.

Left: Originally a farmhouse, now an outstanding country inn, with a variety of sumptuous guest rooms.

GLENDEVEN, 8221 North Highway 1, Little River, CA 95456; (707) 937-0083; Jan and Janet deVries, Innkeepers. An idyllic 7-room guest house 2 miles south of Mendocino on the rugged north coast. Private baths and shared baths. Open all year. Rates, including Continental breakfast: $45 to $70 double; single $10 less. No other meals served. Children accepted at discretion of innkeepers. No pets. No credit cards accepted. Hiking, nature walks in immediate vicinity and in nearby state park.

DIRECTIONS: Inn is on Route 1, north of Van Damme State Park, just 2 miles south of Mendocino and north of the small village of Little River.

Oceanside retreat to luxury

For such an elegant establishment, Heritage House has had an unusually racy past. It was built in 1877 by the grandfather of the present innkeeper for a lumberman who used the cove at the base of the cliffs as a shipping point for redwood ties. Over the years it came to have less honorable uses. Illegal aliens, primarily Asians who provided cheap labor for building the railroads in the late 1800s, were dropped off by the boatload; and during Prohibition, the cove was a virtual marina for rumrunners.

When Don Dennen and his wife were visiting the area in 1949, they found the house battered and abandoned but still boasting the graceful lines and fine craftsmanship of the "State of Maine" architecture so typical of northern California in Don's grandfather's time. The setting was spectacular. In an area where panoramic ocean views are commonplace, the house has an unmatched vista of cliffs, cove, rocks, and ocean. Don recalls they made arrangements "within the hour" to buy the place, and he and his wife set about creating Heritage House.

The original house provided the nucleus, and other structures were added, with luxurious touches everywhere. The lounge, spacious and heavy-beamed, was originally an apple-storage house, which they bought and reassembled after carting it twenty-four miles. It has a huge fireplace, comfortable easy chairs, and round oak tables. The sun-dappled dining room, joining the lounge to the main house, has a window wall with views of the rocky cove below. The food consists of well-prepared American cooking, from the excellent soups and beautifully presented appetizers to the lovely dessert tortes and parfaits. The Saturday night buffet featuring prime ribs is deservedly popular, and the bite-size hotcakes from Mrs. Dennen's own recipe are a must at breakfast.

The limited number of guest rooms in the main building has been supplemented by cottages tucked

Heritage House is a complex of simple buildings with luxurious interiors. OVERLEAF: Two of the cottages, *above*. The right one has a sod roof for coolness. The extensive grounds, *below*, have many attractions of their own.

away on the hillside. One unit has a sod roof, and all have been carefully placed on the landscaped grounds to provide an unobstructed view. Two of the spacious and luxurious newer units are La Maison 2, an elegant suite furnished with antiques, and the Water Tower, a duplex with a two-story living room and a balcony guests can sleep on.

Almost any country inn represents a retreat from the world ouside. Usually it is a retreat to a simpler way of life, but at Heritage House it is a retreat to luxury.

HERITAGE HOUSE, 5200 Highway 1, Little River, CA 95456; (707) 937-5885; L. D. Dennen, Innkeeper. A luxurious 52-room inn on the north coast of Calif. Private baths. Open Feb. through Nov. Rates: $70 to $128 single; $90 to $132 double; Sitting room suite $148 double. Additional guest in room $40. Rates include dinner and breakfast. Dining room open to the public by reservation. Children welcome. No pets. No credit cards accepted. Tennis and golf available nearby.

DIRECTIONS: Inn is on Rte. 1 in Little River, 5 miles north of intersection of Routes 128 and 1.

VICTORIAN FARMHOUSE

Little River — NORTH COAST

Where quiet reigns amid Victorian splendor

People come here to get away from the hustle and bustle of everyday living and to relax. Tom and Jane Szilasi make it happen. No phones, no radio, no TVs, and no clocks in the rooms—just a local paper left around that comes out once a week. Here you can see the Pacific Ocean from the front porch and smell sweet flowers and herbs in the gardens.

The area is unique. You might think you were on the coast of Ireland or New England if you didn't see redwoods. Coasts, coves, and rocks are part of God's wilderness. There are no traffic lights. "You don't see what you breathe" and "The area hasn't been spoiled by the fast-food chains," the Szilasi's point out.

"You feel like you're going to grandma's," is how Tom feels about the place. It's that comfortable. Pictures of his family, back to his great grandparents,

Left: This ground-floor guest suite has a sitting room and private garden entrance.

hang on the walls, some in the original old frames from Hungary. The living room is decorated with oak and early American furnishings, and the guest rooms are filled with French-Victorian pieces.

Sometimes, when Tom goes out, he comes back to find guests playing backgammon in front of the fireplace or sipping sherry in the garden. For a man who gave up being sales manager at Johnson and Johnson and having to live on a plane, it's nice to be home!

THE VICTORIAN FARMHOUSE, 7001 Highway One, P.O. Box 357, Little River, CA 95456; (707) 937-0697; Tom and Jane Szilasi, Innkeepeers. This 1877 Victorian farmhouse has 4 guest rooms in the house and 2 in "The Caretaker's Cottage," all with private baths and queen or king-size beds. Open all year. Rates, including Continental breakfast: $55. No other meals served but there are many fine restaurants in the area. Each room provided with a hot pot and ingredients for a cup of tea or coffee. No children under 16. No pets. No credit cards accepted. Walks and picnicing on the grounds and croquet in the summer.

DIRECTIONS: 3 miles south of Mendocino on Rte. 1.

Hollywood set piece on a rugged coast

Built on an oceanside landscape of high bluffs and steep coastal slopes, the village of Elk, on the rugged northern coast of California, seems as isolated and remote as it is beautiful. Elk had its beginning as a prosperous lumber camp, where dizzying trestles, connecting the mainland to the huge offshore rocks sculpted by the sea, were used to load lumber from the nearby Albion forests onto schooners bound for San Francisco.

In 1917, the Goodyear Lumber Company built Harbor House as a guest lodge for entertaining corporate executives and customers. A larger version of the redwood model house built for the Panama-Pacific International Exposition in 1915, it was a company showpiece. Built on a cliff, Harbor House faces Elk's most imposing seascape, a cove with craggy promontories and rocks tunneled by the sea that look like the inspiration for some of Henry Moore's sculptures.

Innkeeper Pat Corcoran administers Harbor House with a sure and somewhat autocratic hand. "For breakfast," she explains, "guests are likely to get whatever I'm in the mood to cook. I do serve substantial dinners. Good soups, then local fish or a chicken dish or some rather good stuffed pork chops, and the freshest vegetables I can find. But I outdo myself with the desserts—I specialize in tortes." The food has to be good. It competes with a dining room panorama of the cove and a stunning view of every Pacific sunset.

The style at Harbor House is ruggedly casual. "The climb down the cliff to our private beach is not simply a nice civilized jaunt," says Pat, "so I can be pretty sure my guests aren't going to go bird-watching in white flannels."

The guest rooms in the main house have the atmosphere of Hollywood versions of executive retreats. One upstairs room, in green and white, is half the length of a sound stage, with large beds, triple-

mirrored vanities and chaises longues. Downstairs is an even larger wood-paneled room, really a suite, with a well-stocked library of books on nature, ecology, and geology.

The vast redwood-paneled living room has an Edwardian flavor, with lots of good magazines, a piano, and perhaps the world's largest collection of guitar records beside the stereo. Harbor House manages to be both formal and casual at the same time, a unique building in a stunning setting.

Expansiveness is the word to describe Harbor House, from the ocean view, left, *to the cedar-paneled lounge,* above, *to the luxurious guest room,* overleaf.

HARBOR HOUSE, 5600 South Highway 1, P.O. Box 369, Elk, CA 95432; (707) 877-3203; Pat Corcoran, Innkeeper. A unique 5-room inn, with 4 cottages, on a high bluff above a spectacular ocean cove. Private baths. Fireplaces in most rooms, Franklin stoves in cottages. Open all year. Rates: $90 to $125 double, including dinner and breakfast served to overnight guests only; each additional person in same accommodation $25. Children not encouraged. Pets allowed in cottages. No credit cards accepted. Private beach in cove down a cliff path. Fishing and skin diving nearby.

DIRECTIONS: Inn is 17 miles south of Mendocino on Rte. 1, just north of the village of Elk, midway between Mendocino and Point Arena.

Handcrafted triumph, unique among inns

St. Orres is as much a triumph of the spirit as one of design. Its complex array of ornate domes is not, as one might expect, the work of the nineteenth-century Russian settlers in northern California, but the creation of two contemporary American master carpenters. Richard Wasserman and Eric Black bought a dilapidated fishing lodge and went to work. With the help of their friends, they built their own design around it, doing almost everything by hand, piece by piece, room by room. They were strongly influenced by the buildings constructed by Russian trappers in the late 1800s, but their creation went far beyond a nineteenth-century frontier house.

As do all good carpenters, Richard and Eric love the feel of a fine piece of wood. The inn's exterior is of Oregon red cedar, and the interiors are paneled in tongue-and-groove redwood. They are proud that many of the excellent materials used are recycled: the heavy frame of the inn itself is made from timbers salvaged from an old sawmill, and the copper on the domes is the discarded cladding of computer control equipment. Quality was an all-important consideration and construction was slow; but when they opened in 1977, Richard and Eric had one of the most unusual inns in America, with stunning visual effects both inside and out. A massive stone fireplace in the sitting room stands opposite a wall of six California oak doors, each with matching stained-glass windows made by a local craftsman. The dining room ends in a three-story tower with more stained glass encircling the dome. The eight guest rooms have redwood paneling in different geometric tongue-and-groove designs, and the built-in beds are covered with striking custom-made velvet quilts. Each guest room has a specially designed closet combining both chest and wardrobe. Even the telephone booth at St. Orres is paneled with redwood.

The food is excellent, and many visitors make the lovely drive all the way from San Francisco along the winding coast just for dinner. Others come for St. Orres' wonderful natural setting and feeling of isolation. Waves crash against the rocks in the craggy

Left: The tower, with its dome and stained glass, is an exceptional place to dine. OVERLEAF: The handmade inn, with its dining tower on the right.

Each of the guest rooms has tongue-and-groove redwood walls in varying designs. The quilts are handmade locally.

cove opposite the inn, and the inn's own beach, the next cove up, is a protected curve of sand at the mouth of a creek.

Eventually, the innkeeper-carpenters will build cabins in the thirty-five acres of redwood forest behind the inn, and the structures will be planned with the same deliberate care and mature imagination that went into St. Orres itself. No one plans to rush things.

ST. ORRES, P.O. Box 523, Gualala, CA 95445; (707) 884-3303; Eric Black, Rick Wasserman, Rosemary Campiformio, Ted Black, Innkeepers. A strikingly handsome 8-room inn on the north coast, lovingly built by hand by the proprietors. Shared baths. Rates: $45 to $55 double or single, including Continental breakfast. Write or phone for reservations and rates in newly constructed cabins with wood-burning Franklin stoves and private baths. Dining room open every day, year round except Tuesday. Sunday brunch. Children welcome. No pets. Visa, MasterCard accepted. Private beach. Hiking.

DIRECTIONS: On Rte. 1, 106 miles north of San Francisco, 2 miles north of Gualala.

TIMBER COVE INN

Jenner   **NORTH COAST**

A romantic inn in Ansel Adams' country

Timber Cove is in Ansel Adams' country and Ansel Adams is in Timber Cove. Hanging in the lobby are photographs he took of the Sonoma coast when he visited his friend, Richard Clements, who designed and built this "Innkeepers' Inn."

Adams' picture of the inn's reflecting pool is the key to Timber Cove. It is a place that invites peaceful quiet and contemplation. The environment is carefully controlled to do just that and it never falters. There is no telephone or TV.

Romantic is the other mood, and in creating this ambience the present innkeepers, the Hojohns, have more than succeeded. Glowing candelabras, a pulsating fire, and flute and classical guitar music heighten the senses. At a table for two in the restaurant, you can whisper sweet nothings while glimpsing the ocean.

Rising seven stories above rocks behind the inn is a sculpture by Beniamino Bufano, dedicated to world peace. The torso in the pool is his also, a gift because he loved the setting. Art is highly regarded here and Carroll Hojohn's shop at the inn features quality art and crafts made of indigenous materials by local artists.

The Hojohns have been remodeling the guest rooms; nearly all are complete. Baths are fitted with hot tubs or Roman soaking tubs and look out on the ocean. If you're looking for the ultimate in luxury, try the Timber Cove Inn.

TIMBER COVE INN, Coast Hwy. 1, Jenner, CA 95450; (707) 847-3231; Richard and Carroll Hojohn, Innkeepers. Massive but modern open redwood-beam construction offers panoramic views of the northern Sonoma coast from most of the inn's 42 rooms. Rates: $48 to $125. All have showers or baths; about ⅔ have fireplaces. Twin, double, queen, and king-size beds. Children limited. $5 charge for pets. Excellent restaurant with Continental menu. Full bar. Open all year except Dec. 24 and 25. Visa, MasterCard accepted. Reserve well in advance for weekends. Excellent gift shop.

DIRECTIONS: 3 miles north of Fort Ross on Rte. 1 or 28 miles north of Bodega Bay.

Watch for the distinctive sign on the winding Coast highway.

Enticing Czech-Viennese cuisine

It's a long way from post-war Czechoslovakia to the little town of Inverness on the California coast, and its's an interesting story, which Manka and Milan Prokupek might tell you some day. The end of the story is the delightful country inn they started in 1955, where they serve their wonderful Czech-Viennese cuisine that entices guests from all parts of California to the plain but comfortable dining room where service is best described as "European elegance."

Dinner always begins at the buffet table with fruit, cheese, cold meats, and salads. A hot soup follows and a choice of eight entrées, of which roast duckling with caraway or fresh oysters from Tomales Bay are usually the favorites. Finally the delicate Czech pastries arrive, especially prepared by Manka's hand. Guests can still enjoy the mocha meringue that originally made her famous.

When Milan Jr. and his wife Judy agreed to manage Inverness Lodge, the Prokupeks were delighted. The town really became a Czech enclave when their daughter and son-in-law opened a restaurant nearby, Vladimirs, with emphasis on Moravian-Czech cooking.

INVERNESS LODGE, P.O. Box 126, Inverness, CA 94937; (415) 669-1034; Milan and Judith Prokupek, Innkeepers. A turn-of-the-century brown-shingled house in a grove of oak and acacia, with 4 guest rooms, 2 with sun decks and 1 with fireplace. Five additional rooms in a separate cottage. Dining room, serving Czech specialties, overlooks the garden. Pastries, served from a heavily-laden dessert cart, are expertly prepared by Manka. Rates: $32.50 to $45 double. Children by prior arrangement. No pets. Closed Tuesday and Wednesday all year. November through May, open weekends only. Reservations required. Restaurant open for breakfast and dinner. Visa, MasterCard, American Express accepted.

DIRECTIONS: North on Rte. 1 to Point Reyes Station, just before bridge, then west and north again to Inverness. At the sign "Manka's Restaurant" turn left up the hill a short way to the Lodge.

The top-floor windows of the famous dining room overlook the colorful garden.

A country inn that is truly blessed

Because it once was rumored that a ghost inhabited this house, inn proprietors Mary Davies and Stephen Kimball had the local Episcopal priest bless each room with holy water. Only good spirits live there now and peaceful is the word used most often to describe Ten Inverness Way.

Built as a modest residence in 1904, the redwood-shingled house was remodeled by Kimball in 1980 into a bed and breakfast. The large fir-paneled living room has antique furnishings and an oriental rug. Guests gather in the evening to sip sherry near the stone fireplace and pedal out tunes on the player piano. Bowls of cut flowers grown in the gardens enliven all the rooms.

The five guest rooms that were family bedrooms still have a homey feeling. They share two baths. Mary, who acts as resident innkeeper, serves a full breakfast in the corner dining room, with Danish fireplace. The menu varies at the whim of the cook but count on banana pancakes, quiche, or cheese-scrambled eggs, the house specialties.

TEN INVERNESS WAY, Inverness, CA 94937; (415) 669-1648; Ruth Kalter, Mary Davies, and Stephen Kimball, Innkeepers. The inn has 5 guest rooms sharing 2 baths. Open all year but closed Mondays in winter. Rates, including full breakfast and tax: $43 single; $48 double. One with twin beds and 4 with double beds. Children welcome. No pets. No credit cards accepted. Excellent restaurants in the immediate vicinity. Nearby is Point Reyes National Seashore. Birdwatch on the bay, or hike and horseback ride in the parks.

DIRECTIONS: From San Francisco US 101 to San Anselmo-Sir Francis Drake Blvd. exit and continue on Sir Francis Drake to Olema. Right on Rte. 1 and follow signs to Inverness. At Inverness Inn Restaurant, turn left to Ten Inverness Way.

The sunny breakfast room.

OLEMA INN

In a tiny village filled with sunshine

Donn Downing, a former reporter for *Time* magazine, and Eugene Wedell, the architect who saved the Olema Inn from demolition, are responsible for the changing fortunes of this inn. Built as a saloon in 1876, it functioned as a bank and stagecoach stop before becoming a hotel. It also served as a GI barracks during World War II.

Wedell's restoration of the New England colonial inn is extraordinary, down to the elegant wooden molding around the windows. Downings's wife Letitia has decorated the interior with early American furnishings and period wallpapers. Second floor guest rooms share breakfast in the upstairs parlor that acts as a gallery for local artists.

There are three dining rooms sharing a chef trained in Nouvelle Cuisine, all offering a variety of fish dishes, as well as beef, duck, and veal—fresh food that is obtained locally. On weekends, chamber music accompanies meals.

Although fifty-five people live in the village, nearly one million pass by annually on the way to spectacular Point Reyes National Seashore. Buffered by the Inverness Ridge, there is no costal fog here. It is always sunny at The Olema Inn.

THE OLEMA INN, P.O. Box 10, Olema, CA 94950; (415) 663-8441; Donn and Letitia Downing and Eugene Wedell, Owners. Three guest rooms, 1 with private bath, 2 with shared baths. Rates, including full breakfast: $50 to $60 week days, $60 to $70 weekends. Restaurant open daily except Wednesdays for luncheon and dinner; Sunday brunch 10 A.M. to 3 P.M. Bar open (beer and wine only) 11:30 A.M. to 10 P.M. Children welcome. No pets. Visa, MasterCard accepted.

DIRECTIONS: From San Francisco Rte. 1 to San Anselmo-Sir Francis Drake Blvd. exit. Continue on Sir Francis Drake to Olema. Inn is at intersection with Rte. 1.

Only wine, beer, coffee, and orange juice are served at the bar.

HOLLY TREE INN

Right in the middle of the countryside

"As a country person, I think when you visit a city it's important to know what the surrounding countryside looks like," said Diane Balogh, keeper of the Holly Tree Inn. "Our inn is the perfect place for visitors to San Francisco who would also like to discover the countryside." Situated in the midst of one of America's most beautiful natural landscapes, the Holly Tree is the perfect base of operation while exploring and absorbing the rare beauty of Marin County. Built in 1939 by a Swedish immigrant, the inn, with its solid beamed ceiling and white paneled walls, feels like one of Swedish artist Karl Larssen's winsome paintings. Crisp flower prints cover comfortable easy chairs, and area rugs warm polished wooden floors. Both complement the feeling of simplicity dictated by the northern European architecture and its wooded setting. The living room, dominated by a rustic stone hearth, and the adjoining dining room, with its cozy reading nook in front of a second, free-standing fireplace, are flanked by the inn's four guest rooms, each offering a view of the surrounding forest.

HOLLY TREE INN, 3 Silverhills Road, Box 642, Point Reyes Station, CA 94956; (415) 663-1554; Diane and Tom Balogh, Innkeepers. Surrounded by beautiful countryside, this inn offers 4 guest rooms, 2 with private baths and 2 sharing. Double, twin, or king-size beds. Rates: $55 to $65, including a Continental breakfast weekdays and a more generous breakfast on weekends. $10 charge for 3rd person in same room. Sherry served in the evening. No other meals served. Children welcome. No pets. No credit cards accepted. The surrounding area offers a variety of activities including fishing, nature walks, bicycling or beachcombing. Open all year.

DIRECTIONS: From San Francisco, US 101 north to San Anselmo-Sir Francis Drake Blvd exit. At Olema, turn right onto Rte. 1. At sign for Inverness, turn left onto Sir Francis Drake Blvd. Take first left onto Bear Valley Road (unmarked). Take first right onto Silverhills Road (unmarked), look for "Holly Tree" sign, turn right then go left to inn.

A view from the sitting room, looking into the dining room.

Cherished family home; gracious country inn

Most people, when their children grow up and start living on their own, begin to think about moving into a smaller home and taking it easy. But not Gene and Ann Swett. When one after another of their six children moved away from the Swetts' ample Tudor-style home, they took in foreign exchange students to fill each gap.

"This has always been a very special house," says Ann. "It is the sort of place where strangers arrive at the door and ask if they can come in to look around. We just like to have it filled all the time."

And so the Swetts decided to go all the way and convert their home into a small inn. First, they toured the state, visiting other inns in order to pick and choose among their favorite features. They opened in September 1978, and the Old Monterey Inn quickly became known as a gracious country inn that could stand comparison with the finest in the area.

Each of the ten guest rooms has its own distinctive flair, whether it's a cozy treetop chamber with a private sitting room or a secluded cottage complete with fireplace and bay windows that open onto the formal rose garden. The house is constructed in such a cunning fashion that even when it is filled with guests, quiet and privacy prevail. A stay at this inn is so comfortable and intimate it's like visiting old friends.

In the evening a large tray of condiments served "curry-style" with cream cheese and crackers attracts all to the living room. There, over a glass of wine or sherry, guests share their day or gain from the experiences of the Swetts who are both travel guides *par excellence*. But the principal occasion at the Old Monterey Inn is breakfast. Served in front of a crackling fire in the dining room or, when the weather is fine, in the sun-dappled garden, this gentle repast is conducive to happy talk and new friendship. Rich and fragrant coffee, orange juice afloat with banana slices, and artistically arranged fresh fruit or a compote begin the morning. If Gene's been busy in the

Left: An elegant setting for breakfast, to start the day.

The guest rooms were done by a decorator, with additional, personal touches by the innkeepers.

kitchen you might be treated to his famous popovers. He attributes their giant size to *very* fresh eggs.

But what truly makes this inn stand out among the rest is the Swetts' mutual dedication to infinite detail. You see it and feel it everywhere. And this, finally, is what makes an inn great.

OLD MONTEREY INN, 500 Martin St., Monterey, CA 93940, (408) 375-8284; Gene and Ann Swett, Innkeepers. Handsome Tudor-style family home, now a 10-room inn in one of California's most scenic areas. Private and semi-private baths. Open all year. A generous Continental breakfast is the only meal served. Rates: $100 to $170 single or double. Children over 16 welcome. No pets. No credit cards accepted. All popular sports facilities nearby; deep-sea fishing, whale watching; 5 minutes from picturesque Carmel; short drive to John Steinbeck's Cannery Row and the famed 17-Mile Drive.

DIRECTIONS: From San Francisco take Rte. 1 to Monterey Peninsula. Take the Munras exit from Rte. 1. Turn left on Soledad then right on Pacific. Go approximately 6 blocks to Martin.

GOSBY HOUSE INN

Pacific Grove — MONTEREY

International flavor in a seaside inn

Pacific Grove, on California's beautiful Monterey Peninsula, began as a Methodist retreat whose residents lived in tents. As the town's imposing Victorian architecture testifies, however, the good townsmen soon wanted more elaborate accommodations. The Gosby House Inn on Lighthouse Avenue is a particularly fine example of their elevated taste in architecture. Built of redwood, turreted and gabled in the fashion of the 1880s, the Gosby House Inn was the result of a local handyman's bid for the visitors who came to bathe or to be uplifted by the lectures.

By the time Roger and Sally Post came upon it, however, it had become a shabby establishment whose fortunes had not survived Pacific Grove's evolution from a nineteenth-century camp to a modern resort community. The Posts, with the help of young hotelman Bill Patterson, began a complete restoration. Dropped ceilings were removed to reveal exquisite plaster rosettes in the original ceiling above; stripping and cleaning disclosed elaborate patterns in the brass hardware. Slowly, the fine old mansion began to reappear.

When the basic restoration had been finished, Bill began to think about furniture. For more than a month, he lived in the house, sleeping in each guest room "to find out what it needed, what kind of bed, how it should be placed." He brought in European-style furnishings from the turn of the century, a time when the popularity of the Gosby House Inn was at its height, to create a California inn with an international flavor.

The predominant color scheme is light and airy, and white ruffled curtains temper the strong sunlight of the seaside town. Each room is named for a prominent local figure; guests may choose the Robert Louis Stevenson Room or the John Steinbeck Room. Whatever the accommodation, it will be distinctive, because the eccentric construction of the house has created rooms with odd corners and projecting bays. Perhaps the most dramatic is the turret room, with a curving window wall that affords a view toward the water over the lower town. Guests enjoy a Continental breakfast in the common room, with its heavy, dark oak table and Queen Anne chairs. In a huge armoire, Sally Post has arranged a delightful collection of antique dolls.

Pacific Grove, with its wealth of Victorian cottages set amid blooming gardens, combines nineteenth-century charm with enough present-day excitement to please a whole new generation of visitors who could not do better than to put up at the Gosby House Inn.

Left: A corner of the common room, with Mrs. Post's collection of antique dolls.

GOSBY HOUSE INN, 643 Lighthouse Ave., Pacific Grove, CA 93950; (408) 375-1287; Ralph and Kit Sotzing, Innkeepers. A charming architectural oddity, with 18 rooms, in a Victorian seaside community on Monterey Bay. Private and shared baths. Open all year. Rates, including Continental breakfast: $45 to $65 double. No restaurant, but menus for area restaurants available for guests' convenience. Children not encouraged. No pets. No credit cards accepted. Inn is 6 blocks from the ocean. Golfing, tennis, and sailing nearby.

DIRECTIONS: South of Monterey on Rte. 1, take Pebble Beach-Pacific Grove exit onto Rte. 68 west, which becomes Forest Ave. Proceed on Forest to Lighthouse Ave. Turn left on Lighthouse 3 blocks to inn at 18th Street.

GREEN GABLES INN

A part-time country inn

For three months of the year innkeepers Roger and Sally Post turn their own home into a country inn. Built in 1888, Green Gables, a lovely old period house-by-the-sea, rests on the coastline of Pacific Grove, a community noted for fine old homes. Consider yourself lucky to have booked one of its three available guest rooms, for the Posts are deeply dedicated to innkeeping. They are the owners of nearby Gosby House and have recently acquired Stonehouse Inn in Carmel.

Decorated with antique furnishings, the inn's living room has large bay-window alcoves and an unusual fireplace, framed by stained-glass panels that cast a roseate glow. Before guests depart for dinner, they can have late-afternoon tea in front of a cheery fire.

Of the three available bedrooms that share a bath, there is the Balcony Room, with an ocean view and sitting area, the Gable Room, with an ocean and town view, and the Garret Room, with a window seat overlooking the town. Guests wake up to a generous Continental breakfast served in a dining room facing the sea. The Seventeen Mile Drive, Pebble Beach, Carmel, and John Steinbeck's famous Cannery Row are all nearby.

GREEN GABLES INN, 104 Fifth St., Pacific Grove, CA 93950; (408) 375-2095; Roger and Sally Post, Innkeepers. Three guest rooms with shared bath. The inn is open only during June, July, and August; prospective guests are urged to make reservations well in advance. Rates: $70 to $75 single or double. A Continental breakfast is included in the rate. There are many excellent restaurants as well as recreational facilities in the area: golf courses, ocean beaches, pine woods, and historic sites. No smoking inside the inn.

DIRECTIONS: From Rte. 1 exit on Rte. 68 west to Pacific Grove. Continue on Forest Ave. to Ocean View Blvd., then turn right to 5th Ave.

The view of Green Gables was photographed by George Allen.

Proof that dreams can come true

"We made it happen because it was our dream—we wanted to do it," says Dick Stewart, one of the innkeepers. The story of this inn is a dream come true. Ten years ago, Dick and his partner, Bob Alberson, stayed at Happy Landing after failing to get a room at the place they usually went to. Falling in love with it, they returned there year after year and finally decided to make it their own. For five years they relentlessly pursued the owner, until he agreed to sell them the place.

The new innkeepers have made "happiness" the theme of the inn. Champagne marks guests' birthdays, and there is a decanter of sherry in each room to celebrate any occasion that may arise. Place card holders in the rooms provide a variety of proverbs to ponder over, such as "Happy is the house that shelters a friend" and "Happiness is catching."

The complex is made up of three pink-stuccoed buildings that encircle a gazebo and fish pond, and each of the cathedral-ceilinged guest rooms opens onto this courtyard. "When you open the curtain, between eight and ten, that's our signal for breakfast," the innkeepers tell the guests. A knock on the door often finds guests sitting in bed waiting for the wonderful homemade muffins or carrot bread, fresh juice or strawberries, and coffee brought on wicker trays.

HAPPY LANDING INN, Monte Verde between 5th and 6th, P.O. Box 2619, Carmel-by-the-Sea, CA 93921; (408) 624-7917; Bob Alberson and Dick Stewart, Innkeepers. Cathedral-ceilinged rooms open onto a beautiful garden courtyard; 7 with private baths, 2 share bath. Double, queen, and twin beds. One room has a wood-burning fireplace. Open all year. Rates: $40 to $65 double, including Continental breakfast. Children over 12 welcome. No pets. Visa, MasterCard, American Express accepted. Two blocks to Ocean Ave. and numerous specialty shops, restaurants, and galleries. Bicycling, tennis, and golf in the area.

DIRECTIONS: North of Ocean Ave. on Monte Verde between 5th and 6th.

The relaxing garden courtyard at twilight.

PINE INN

Carmel's first country inn

Country innkeeping came to Carmel in 1902, when the Pine Inn opened. Built to house prospective land buyers, it prospered and the old Duckworth Hotel had to be put on rollers and added onto it. But one thing never changed: the personal warmth and service that have always come first. The McKee family, which owns the inn, is rightfully proud of that.

It is not surprising that the inn is decorated with elegant Victorian furnishings, having opened the year after Queen Victoria died. There are touches of opulence everywhere: a Tiffany glass canopy over the door to the Red Parlor; the Gazeboé Room's domed roof that rolls back to uncover the sky.

Dining in the deep-red carpeted dining rooms can be provocative because of unusual dishes like Abalone Steak, Veal Oscar, and Beef Wellington. Friday night's seafood buffet and Sunday's Champagne brunch are truly enticing!

After a bit of the bubbly, you may feel like taking a nap. No two bedrooms here are the same. The ones in the older part of the inn are small, but abundant in charm and period furnishings. Freshly-cut flowers abound, adding a touch of natural beauty to an inn where hospitality is a way of life.

PINE INN, Box 250, Ocean Ave. and Monte Verde, Carmel-by-the-Sea, CA 93921; (408) 624-3851; Carroll M. McKee, Innkeeper. The inn's Victorian atmosphere is enhanced by period furnishings and fresh flowers. The Gazeboé, an indoor garden dining room, has a dome that opens to the sky. Full-service dining room offers meals daily, and the Friday-night seafood buffet and Sunday Champagne brunch are popular. Inn has 49 rooms with private baths. Rates: standard doubles $48 to $55; superior doubles and twins $55 to $64; queen $52 to $65; king $70 to $95. Children welcome. No pets. Open all year. Reservations at least 1 month ahead. Visa, MasterCard, American Express accepted.

DIRECTIONS: From Rte. 1 west on Ocean Avenue to Monte Verde.

CYPRESS INN

A strong Spanish influence

The Cypress Inn, also owned by the McKee family, is a reminder of days when the Spanish flag flew over the Monterey Peninsula. Red-tiled and towered, the inn takes you back to the early Spanish explorers and Franciscan missionaries who gave Carmel so much of its flavor.

Past the inn's stately entrance hall and through an arched doorway, you enter the white-stuccoed living room. A high-beamed ceiling, wrought-iron chandelier, and fireplace tell part of the story, but the courtyard tells the rest. Peaceful and secluded, you experience the same inspiration and solitude that lured writers like Jack London and Sinclair Lewis to Carmel.

Across from the inn is the Church of the Wayfarer, a place well worth visiting. A biblical garden has been planted in front, where fig, date, palm, and olive trees, and St. John's bread and cypress hedges—the plants of the bible—grow. People say the garden thrives because the climate is the same as that of the Holy Land. The Cypress Inn is a bit of paradise in Carmel-by-the-Sea.

CYPRESS INN P.O. Box Y, Carmel-by-the-Sea, CA 93921; (408) 624-3871; the McKee family, Innkeepers. This elegant and comfortable Spanish-style inn has 33 guest rooms, with private baths, phones, and color TV. Rates: $45 to $75, including Continental breakfast. Twin, double, queen, and king-size beds available. There is no restaurant in the inn, nor does it serve liquor, but there are many attractive restaurants and numerous bars in Carmel. Children welcome. No pets. Reservations must be made six weeks in advance. Visa, MasterCard, American Express accepted.

DIRECTIONS: One block south of Ocean Avenue, at Lincoln and Seventh, in the heart of Carmel.

VAGABOND HOUSE

Carmel   MONTEREY

A garden retreat western style

Clocks are everywhere.

The heart of this romantic hideaway—its outdoor living room—is the plant-filled garden courtyard shaded by two California live oaks. Gigantic staghorn ferns, tree fuchsias, camellia bushes, and cyclamens flourish, and the permanent evergreens provide a background for the seasonal floral changes.

Built in 1941 as a series of efficiency apartments and converted to an inn in 1947, Vagabond House presents itself from the outside as a group of neat white-stuccoed cottages built into the side of a gently rising hill. A curving path leads up into the courtyard in the center of the complex.

Innkeepers Dennis Levett and Jewell Brown have redecorated the rooms with new rugs and bedspreads and supplemented the original collection of antiques with many fine examples of their own, particularly in a handsome new lobby enhanced by a magnificent oriental rug. Every room has one or more clocks, many of them collectors' pieces.

The guest rooms are spacious and all have private baths. Some have fireplaces; others have kitchens. Every room either opens directly onto the garden or overlooks it. The inn is open all year, and many guests settle in for a week, a month, or a whole season. Each room is decorated in an individual and sometimes whimsical style, often with odd curios from the past, but somehow the effect is always harmonious and pleasing. All the rooms are unusually well stocked with books ranging from 1930s hardcover mysteries, anthologies, and back issues of the *National Geographic* to recent novels and nonfiction. A decanter of cream sherry in each room provides a hospitable touch.

Service at Vagabond House is informal but gracious and attentive. In the morning, guests open their doors to the day's *San Francisco Chronicle,* and walk through the garden to the reception room to pick up their Continental breakfasts. Eating in the patio is popular, but many guests prefer to take their breakfasts back to their rooms on a tray. No other meals are served, but Carmel abounds in a wide variety of fine eating places.

VAGABOND HOUSE INN, 4th and Dolores, P.O. Box 2747, Carmel-by-the-Sea, CA 93921; (408) 624-7738; Dennis Levett and Jewell Brown, Innkeepers. An 11-room inn in an oceanside resort town. Open all year. Rates range from $50 to $75 double; singles at a 10% discount; including Continental breakfast. Private baths, some full kitchens. Not ideal for children. Pets on leash only. Visa, MasterCard accepted.

DIRECTIONS: Take Carmel exits off Rte. 1. Drive down Ocean Avenue to Dolores, turn right. Inn is 2½ blocks up on the right.

On the beach.

Where legend lives on

Back in 1905 the Holiday Guest House was the summer home of a Stanford professor. For twenty years, students attended seminars there until it changed owners and became an inn.

During the mid-forties, and for the next twenty-five years, the inn's reputation soared. The legendary Edith Jamison, a New England school teacher, bought it and made quite a name for herself. She served breakfast on dainty little dishes and made sure there was a napkin on everyone's knees. She scolded when there were crumbs on the floor, and the guests loved her. They returned year after year to see her and to enjoy the camellias, columbine, and sweet peas that thrived in her garden.

For the last five years, the Westons have run the inn. It is homey, comfortable, and quiet. The antique pieces they own are easy to live with. A butter churn is used as a bedside table in one of the guest rooms, and a mahogany deck chair from an old cruise ship can be found in another. A French filing cabinet has been converted into a stereo cabinet and bookcase, and is well-stocked with Civil War books and mysteries, Kenneth Weston's favorite reading matter.

Many people still return who were there in Edith Jamison's day. They say she would approve.

HOLIDAY GUEST HOUSE, P.O. Box 234, Carmel-by-the-Sea, CA 93921; (408) 624-6267; Kenneth and Janet Weston, Innkeepers. This turn-of-the-century brown-shingled house has been welcoming guests for over 50 years. Six guest rooms offer a variety of accommodations. Private and shared baths. Some have ocean or garden views. Rates, including a light breakfast: $44 single, $46 double, with private bath; $38 single, $40 double, sharing bath; extra person, in same room $6. No children under 6. No pets. No credit cards accepted. No smoking in the house. A two night minimum for weekends. Open all year. Close to beach, shopping, and dining. The numerous attractions of Carmel and whole of Monterey Peninsula are within easy access.

DIRECTIONS: On Camino Real between Ocean Ave. and 7th.

A secluded, relaxing garden.

STONEHOUSE INN

A fine old house impeccably decorated

Carmel's Stonehouse Inn has the great advantage of being privy to the secrets of a lovely and successful older sister, the Gosby House of Pacific Grove. Quite different from the Gosby, the atmosphere at the Stonehouse conforms to the intimate wooded beauty of Carmel itself. Built in 1906 of hand-shaped stones which were worked by local Indians, the inn is impeccably decorated in shades of sea green and soft apricot, played against sturdy white board-and-batten walls and beamed ceilings. Comfortable wingback chairs, abundant silk flowers and potted plants, and nineteenth-century American prints, artifacts, and toys create a relaxed but refined style. Lodgings range from tiny to moderate, but no matter the size each is pleasing to the eye and quite comfortable. Breakfast, including fresh fruit, fresh-baked croissants, and fruit breads, is served in the glass-enclosed formal dining room, bathed in soft morning light.

STONEHOUSE INN, P.O. Box 2517, Carmel-by-the-Sea, CA 93921; (408) 624-4569; Joseph Smith, Manager. Open all year. Six guest rooms sharing baths. Rates, including Continental breakfast: $60 to $75 double. No other meals served. Numerous fine dining places in Carmel. Sherry and hot apple cider served at the inn. No children under 12. No pets. No smoking. No credit cards accepted.
DIRECTIONS: From Rte. 1 on Ocean Ave. to Monte Verde; turn left to 8th Ave., right on 8th to the inn.

Opulent comfort.

Very relaxed and completely non-plastic

"Very relaxed and completely non-plastic" is how Helen Praeger describes the Mission Ranch. Helen ought to know. She's been working there for seventeen years, as everything from maid to general manager.

Ten blocks outside of bustling Carmel and not surrounded by pavement, the ranch offers a countrified setting with a variety of cottages, well-suited for families. The main house is the original Victorian farmhouse of a dairy, built in 1850, part of the nearby Carmel Mission.

No children, no phones, and no TV keep the farmhouse atmosphere quiet and gracious. Continental breakfast is attended by a hostess who looks after sherry hour too. There are five guest rooms, all furnished with Victorian trappings and all with private baths.

Add to this the tennis courts; a restaurant, open all week, serving fresh Monterey salmon and prime ribs; the old cow barn, with a piano bar and live entertainment and dancing on the weekends, and there is no reason to leave the ranch grounds unless you choose to.

MISSION RANCH, 26270 Dolores, Carmel-by-the-Sea, CA 93923; (408) 624-6643; Helen Praeger, Manager. Adjacent to the Carmel Mission Basilica, the second oldest in California. The inn's towering Cypress and Eucalyptus trees are over 125 years old. Overlooks the Carmel River, the Bay, and scenic Point Lobos. The Victorian main house, with 5 guest rooms, features Continental breakfast and a sherry hour each afternoon. Rates: $63 to $75 double. Guest cottages can accommodate up to 6 persons; all have private baths, telephones, TV, and some kitchenettes. Children and pets by prior arrangement in cottages. Rates average $59.50. Open all year. Visa, MasterCard, American Express accepted. Tennis courts. Excellent restaurant.

DIRECTIONS: Ten blocks south of center of Carmel, at foot of Dolores St.

The old farmhouse at Mission Ranch now welcomes guests for bed and breakfast.

A place to look outward and inward

Ventana resulted from a love affair between Larry Spector, movie producer of *Easy Rider,* and Big Sur. For five years, Spector and architect Kipp Stewart carefully planned and built the inn, 1200 feet above the Pacific, overlooking the ocean for fifty miles in each direction. The site selected bordered on the homes of Big Sur chroniclers Henry Miller and Robinson Jeffers.

Hollywood personalities flocked to Ventana, sometimes for four or five weeks at a time. Steve McQueen, Ali McGraw, Candice Bergen, and Alec Guiness all stayed there, in handsome cedar buildings furnished in modern decor and country elegance. A separate spa building has hot tubs and sauna, and the 90 foot pool offers shelter for nude sun bathers.

Ventana's new owners have made dining newsworthy. The restaurant offers regional fresh fish, marinated leg of lamb, and duck à l'orange, and has garnered the four-star Mobil award. The *Washington Post* hailed its Continental breakfast as the best on the West Coast.

The inn has a romantic ambience and couples are the rule. Those coming from Yugoslavia and Switzerland are reminded of home, but all come to Ventana—"window" in Spanish—to view the marvels of nature and then to look inward.

VENTANA INN, Big Sur, CA 93920; (408) 667-2331; Robert E. Bussinger, Innkeeper. Eight handsome cedar buildings 1200 feet above the Pacific, all with spectacular views. The lobby and public rooms are in the eighth building. The 40 units include 3 duplex Townhouse Suites, each with sitting room, fireplace, and wet bar downstairs; bedroom and bath upstairs. Patchwork quilts and hand-carved and painted headboards make the rooms, all with baths, distinctive. The dining room, with its own special view, is in another house, a walk or drive down the hill. Rates: $125 to $250 double; $15 for 3rd person, including Continental breakfast. Minimum 2-day reservation on weekends. Limited facilities for children. No pets. Jacuzzis, saunas, and heated swimming pool. Visa, MasterCard, American Express accepted. A Boutique specializes in designer clothing, cosmetics, pottery, and writing supplies.
DIRECTIONS: 2½ miles south of Big Sur State Park on Rte. 1. 28 miles south of Carmel.

A modern inn with all the amenities, set in glorious countryside.

DEETJENS BIG SUR INN

Big Sur   **MONTEREY**

Great dining in a Bohemian atmosphere

Deetjens Big Sur Inn is both more and less than an inn. More because metaphysical pursuits are the inn's reason to be. "Grandpa" Helmuth Deetjen, the Norwegian artist who created this roadside oasis in the early 1920s, meant it to be a place of spiritual discovery, and the setting is certainly conducive to this end. The inn, surrounded by towering redwoods, nestled in a sheltering mountain dale, and refreshed by a sparkling stream, has nature as the primary innkeeper. The main building, a weathered, barn-like structure, houses a dining room which offers outstanding food, wine, and classical music and is graced by fine old china, Deetjen's handmade tables and chairs, and an oft-used fireplace. Guest rooms are found in a series of outlying cottages and are filled with beds of varying comfort and relics of past

Left: one of the guest houses on the hillside.

occupants, including dried bridal wreaths, empty wine bottles, and spur-of-the-moment poems. Those who require such amenities as state-of-the-art plumbing and impeccable housekeeping take note—the camp-like atmosphere at this inn does not support such fripperies.

Deetjen's is less than an inn because Ed Gardien, Helmuth Deetjen's protegé and heir, runs it just like Grandpa did. Therefore, no reservations are taken over the phone and, more often than not, no response will be made to written requests for a room.

So how does one stay at the inn? Kismet!

DEETJENS BIG SUR INN, Highway 1, Big Sur, CA 93920; (408) 667-2377; Ed Gardien, Innkeeper. Inn has 16 guest rooms, all in separate cottages with bathrooms. Open all year. Rates range from $28 to $54 double. Dining room open 6 days for full breakfast and dinner. On Tuesdays, Continental breakfast and soup-and-bread dinner only. No bar. Wine available. Guests may bring liquor. Children welcome. No pets. No credit cards accepted. Money order or cashier's check for reservations. The rugged beauty of the Big Sur Wilderness is a great attraction.

DIRECTIONS: On Rte. 1 just south of Nepenthe, Ventana Inn, and Big Sur State Park. On the right, on inside of sharp curve in road.

Innkeeper Ed Gardien, with painting of "Grandpa" Helmuth Deetjen, creator of the inn.

Unbridled spirits
in an Old West hotel

The Union Hotel looks like a nineteenth-century western hotel. Gold-fringed red draperies curtain the archway leading to the large and rather formal dining room. The sitting room's decor includes potted plants and an elaborate mantel, and both rooms share the same florid wallpaper and red carpeting. The bar is hewn from solid African mahogany, and the guest rooms offer transoms numbered in etched glass, sleigh beds with handmade quilts, and a decanter of wine on each dresser. The central upstairs hall has a huge pool table lit by skylights. The patterned floral wallpaper links the rooms and is even on a bathtub. But the Union Hotel is no ordinary nineteenth-century western hotel. It is the somewhat eccentric extension of its vibrant and energetic owner, Dick Langdon.

In 1972, Dick, a highly successful meat wholesaler from Los Angeles, decided it was time to change his lifestyle. He considered buying some ranch property up north but instead wound up buying a hotel, built in 1880 and boarded up for the past nineteen years, in the virtual ghost town of Los Alamos. The antiquing trips for the restoration took a year. Among his unique acquisitions are a pair of two-hundred-year-old Egyptian burial urns, a lamp used in *Gone with the Wind*, headlights from a 1914 Oldsmobile, and a pair of swinging doors from a nineteenth-century New Orleans bordello.

The hotel is open all year, but only on Fridays, Saturdays, and Sundays. "Three days a week is fun," Dick explains. "Beyond that, it becomes work." The first time guests come to the hotel, they can only reserve for one night, because Dick wants to be sure he likes them. All patrons may take a look at the available rooms and choose their own, on a first-come-first-served basis.

There is no menu at the hotel, and guests are served the table d'hôte. It always begins with cheese and crackers and a homemade soup. The most popular is Leather Apron soup, a hearty chicken-and-noodle combination from an old wagon-trail recipe. This is usually followed by a chicken or beef dish, silky-smooth cornbread, and dessert. Dinner is *prix fixe*

Left: The dining room, showing the lush, red color scheme used throughout the inn, as seen, OVERLEAF, in the traditional western bar and in an ornate corner of the lobby.

A guest room off the upstairs hall.

for grownups, but children pay by weight—their own. Dick puts the youngsters on a huge butcher's scale, and the heavier they are, the more their parents pay.

Despite all the excitement and panache at the Union Hotel, Dick and his wife, Teri, like to keep the hotel simple and low-key.

UNION HOTEL, 362 Bell St., Los Alamos, CA 93440; (805) 344-2744; Dick and Teri Langdon, Innkeepers. A 14-room frontier hotel, faithfully restored. Private and shared baths. Open all year, Fridays through Sundays. Rates: $75 to $90 double, with deluxe breakfast of homemade cinnamon rolls, fresh fruit, coffee, and brandy. Restaurant serves dinner only. No children or pets overnight. No credit cards accepted. Croquet, volleyball, badminton. Unexpected period delights, such as a restored 1918 White touring car in which guests may go sightseeing in the area; a reflecting pool that doubles for swimming; a charming Victorian gazebo by day that, at the press of a button, converts to a jacuzzi accommodating 20 guests at night!
DIRECTIONS: From US 101, take Los Alamos turnoff 14 miles north of Buellton, 17 miles south of Santa Maria.

OLD YACHT CLUB, BATH STREET & GLENBOROUGH INNS

Santa Barbara   **SOUTH COAST**

Santa Barbara now has three fine inns

Santa Barbara's gentle climate and captivating beauty have attracted people for centuries. Of those who settled for a time, the Spanish explorers and missionaries left an indelible mark on the character of this city; red tiled roofs and creamy adobe sweep west from the dramatic Santa Ynez mountains to the sea, a vision randomly punctuated by the soft sway of palms. Amidst this idyllic beauty arose three fine bed and breakfast inns. Today, The Old Yacht Club Inn, The Glenborough Inn, and the Bath Street Inn work together in a loose cooperative and offer guests the best of this enchanting city.

One block from the water, THE OLD YACHT CLUB INN was the first to open in the city. Innkeeper Nancy Donaldson is a superb cook who takes pleasure in offering her guests, and those staying at neighboring inns, a satisfying *prix fixe* dinner twice weekly. A trim California craftsman bungalow bedecked with flowers and framed by two matching orange trees, the inn offers visual delight as well as gustatory pleasure. The living room is a harmonious blend of cream, burgundy, and navy with lots of gleaming hardwood peeking out from under Oriental rugs. Bedrooms range from spacious, with private balconies, to small and cozy.

Across town in a residential neighborhood, THE GLENBOROUGH INN is comprised of a 1906 California craftsman bungalow, complete with hot tub, and an 1885 frame cottage just across the street. Jo Ann Bell and Pat Hardy run this inn with an eye to perfection, offering charming, comfortable, and sparkling clean accommodations, fresh bath towels delivered twice daily, an evening turn-down with a pillow mint, and a satisfying breakfast.

Several blocks away, a graceful Queen Anne-style residence houses the BATH STREET INN. Innkeepers Nancy Stover and Susan Brown are drop-outs from the corporate world who have truly found their niche. Says Nancy of her new career, "Innkeeping has

Glenborough Inn guest rooms, *above* and *left*.

restored our faith in humanity. The people we meet here are the kind we really want for friends!" Decorated in fine, traditional furnishings, five comfortable guest rooms are found on the second and third floors, the latter sharing space with a commodious common room filled with game tables, stereo, overstuffed couches, and an extensive library.

THE OLD YACHT CLUB INN, 431 Corona Del Mar, Santa Barbara, CA 93103; (805) 962-1277; Nancy Donaldson, Innkeeper. The inn, an English Tudor-style house built in 1912, has 4 guest rooms sharing 2 baths, 1 with shower, 1 with tub, and wash basins in all rooms. Rates, including complete breakfast: $45 to $70; $10 each extra person. Two night minimum on weekends. Dinner is served 2 nights a week. Beer and wine available for guests. Open all year. No children. No pets. Visa, MasterCard accepted. Smoking in room discouraged, but permitted on porches and in common areas. One block from beach and Sunday art and craft show.

DIRECTIONS: From south on US 101: as you approach Sana Barbara, exit on Cabrillo Blvd. from left lane. Turn left on Cabrillo, continue past bird refuge and Sheraton Hotel to Corona Del Mar and turn right. From north on US 101 to Santa Barbara: at 2nd State St. exit turn right. Turn left on Cabrillo Blvd. Just before Sheraton Hotel turn left on Corona Del Mar.

THE GLENBOROUGH INN, 1327 Bath St., Santa Barbara, CA 93101; (805) 966-0589; Jo Ann Bell and Pat Hardy, Innkeepers. The inn, consisting of 2 houses, has 8 guest rooms; 4 in main house share 2 baths, have double or queen-size beds. Cottage has 2 rooms and 2 suites, all with private baths; one with kitchen. Rates, including breakfast: $55 to $125 double; $5 less single; $10 for each additional person. Open all year. Children not encouraged. No pets. Visa, MasterCard accepted. Smoking and non-smoking rooms. Wine served in evening. Two-night minimum on weekends. Hot tub with complete privacy available.

DIRECTIONS: From Los Angeles, US 101 to Carrillo exit. Right on Carrillo 2 blocks to Bath. Left on Bath 3½ blocks, inn on right. From north, US 101 to Carrillo exit, go left and repeat above.

BATH STREET INN, 1720 Bath St., Santa Barbara, CA 93101; (805) 682-9680; Nancy Stover and Susan Brown, Innkeepers. Five guest rooms, including 1 suite; private and shared baths. Double, king, and extra-long double beds. Open all year. Rates, including generous Continental breakfast, range from $50 to $85 double; $5 less single; $10 each extra person. Port in room and wine each evening. Children not encouraged. No pets. Visa, MasterCard accepted. Off-street parking. Airport or train pickup. Bicycles available. All attractions of Santa Barbara close by.

DIRECTIONS: US 101 to Mission St. exit. East 2 blocks to Bath St., turn right, inn 2½ blocks on left. Parking behind house.

Bath Street Inn sitting room.

Right: The Old Yacht Club Inn.

SAN YSIDRO RANCH

A lush retreat for the status set

San Ysidro Ranch is located on the site of one of a series of missions and way stations Franciscan monks maintained along the California coast in the nineteenth century. The oldest adobe cottage, now kept as a museum, dates from 1826. Its tradition as a way station for weary travelers is still very much alive after more than a century and a half.

It opened as the San Ysidro Ranch in 1893 and was a success almost from the start. John Galsworthy stayed here while making the final revisions on *The Forsyte Saga*. Sinclair Lewis, Somerset Maugham, and Winston Churchill all came here to work in the relaxed atmosphere. For some thirty years before his death in 1958, screen star Ronald Colman owned San Ysidro and used it as an exclusive hideaway for his friends. Bing Crosby and Jack Benny came often. Vivien Leigh and Laurence Olivier were married here, and John F. Kennedy honeymooned at the ranch after his marriage to Jacqueline Bouvier in 1953.

Situated on 540 acres in the hills above Montecito, west of Santa Barbara, the scenery includes views of the Pacific Ocean on one side and the Santa Ynez Mountains on the other. The bridle trails are so

One of the cottages.

extensive that many people stable their own horses at the inn's facilities.

After Colman's death, the ranch changed hands many times; and by 1976, the once-proud estate was badly run down—the landscaping going to seed and the bridle trails choked with undergrowth. Enter Jim Lavenson, former president of the Plaza Hotel in New York City, who took up the banner and saved San Ysidro Ranch. He and his wife, Susie, who is in charge of the interior design, have spent well over $1,300,000 refurbishing the ranch.

All thirty-nine accommodations are private bungalows tucked away in the well-manicured gardens. Always in demand (and most expensive) is the Forest Cottage, which offers both modern furniture and antiques, a whirlpool bath, and a large, secluded redwood deck with complete privacy.

The main house boasts one of the best restaurants in the state. Both steaks and prime ribs are cooked as expertly as the haute cuisine, and Julia Child is a frequent visitor.

Although Jim and Susie are nearing their second million dollars spent on San Ysidro Ranch, they admit the end is not in sight. Perfection is never cheap, but it's always worth it.

An alcove bedroom at Forest Cottage.

Left: Cottages are spread throughout the grounds among impressive trees and plants. OVERLEAF: The intimately lit dining room; the back deck of Forest Cottage; interior of the oldest building, an 1825 adobe cottage preserved as a museum.

SAN YSIDRO RANCH, 900 San Ysidro Lane, Montecito, CA 93108; (805) 969-5046; Jim and Susie Lavenson, Innkeepers. Thirty-eight secluded cottages in beautifully tended gardens. Views of Pacific Ocean and Santa Ynez Mountains. Open all year. Rates: $89 to $298 double. Cribs and rollaway $15 each. Highly rated restaurant serves breakfast, lunch, and dinner. Children welcome. $5 nightly charge for pets. Visa, MasterCard, American Express accepted. Swimming pool, tennis courts, stables, trail rides.

DIRECTIONS: From US 101, exit at San Ysidro Rd., drive east through Montecito Village to San Ysidro Lane.

A collector's paradise by the rolling Pacific

Marjorie Bettenhausen is a dreamer and a dynamo who combines these qualities to make miracles happen. In 1977, she and husband Jack bought a down-and-out 1920s apartment motel in the heart of Seal Beach, just three hundred yards from the shore. Having spent time traveling through Europe, and sharing a love for the inns of the French Riviera, they set out to transform their ugly duckling into a beautiful swan. Today, The Old Seal Beach Inn is a radiant reflection of the Bettenhausen's spirit, as well as a testimony to hard work.

A "chronic collector," Marjorie haunts shops and estate sales searching for just the right furnishings and object d'arts for her inn, which, in her mind, is never quite finished. As she says, "To me this inn is an art form. There's always something that must be added or changed. In a sense I feel like I'm sculpting with a building!" But, to the casual visitor, the inn feels complete.

In the Villa, a wonderful royal blue and rose antique rug blends sumptuously with an antique-velvet bedspread on a cast-iron and brass bed, while the Fuschia room relives the twenties, its original period pieces dressed up in warm, rich colors. The lobby is perfect. It faces a large herringbone brick courtyard and features double French doors dressed with lace sheers, a tile-faced working fireplace, pressed tin ceiling, antique oriental rugs, overstuffed chairs and sofas, brimming bookcases, and lots of flowers.

The entire inn is adorned with blossoms. Ably assisted by a gifted gardener, Jack Bettenhausen is the moving spirit behind the inn's fabulous floral displays. A tall wrought-iron fence imported from France, old-fashioned lamp posts, a cherry-red British telephone booth, and bright aqua awnings complete the scene with color and style.

The inn's vivid personality acts in lively contrasts to the town of Seal Beach, which is a quiet, somewhat

Left: The courtyard, a nice place to relax and meet other guests. A richly decorated guest room.

funky, enclave. If rolls and coffee in the morning aren't quite enough to start the day, a full and hearty breakfast can be found at a locals' hangout just a short stroll away. And for those who prefer a pool to the rolling Pacific, the inn provides a secluded spot for private sunning, as well as complimentary sherry to calm a traveler's cares.

THE OLD SEAL BEACH INN, 212 - 5th St., Seal Beach, CA 90740; (213) 493-2416; Marjorie and Jack Bettenhausen, Innkeepers. The inn has 22 guest rooms, 15 of which have fully equipped kitchens. All have private baths. Beds are double, twin, queen, or king-size. Rates, including Continental breakfast, range from $45 to $100 per room, single or double. Additional guests $7 per day. Open all year. Inquire about winter rates. Children welcome. No pets. Visa, MasterCard, American Express accepted. Inn has swimming pool. Beach 1 block away. Public tennis and golf available. Close to Disneyland.

DIRECTIONS: From Los Angeles south on I-405 to Seal Beach Blvd. exit. Turn left and drive to Pacific Coast Hwy., then right to 3rd light which is 5th St. Turn left. Inn is 2 blocks away on 5th.

Laguna Beach # CARRIAGE HOUSE **SOUTH COAST**

New Orleans style in Laguna Beach

The Carriage House is an historical landmark building situated several blocks from the ocean on a quiet, residential street in Laguna Beach. Dominated by a brick patio garden filled with flowers, lush greenery, caged canaries and finches, and a cool fountain, the inn is shaded overall by a grand carrotwood tree draped with Spanish moss. The two-story, Creole-style structure, which encloses the garden on three sides, is reminiscent of New Orleans architecture.

Six spacious suites comprise the inn, each with its own separate living room and most with two bedrooms and fully equipped kitchens. Each has its own individual style; thus, Lilac Time is a romantic getaway especially favored for its half-canopied brass bed and old fashioned charm, Green Palms seems a world removed with its tropical, airy, and ample dimensions, and Primrose Lane feels like a country house.

Left: No problem with mosquitos in this bed.

The Carriage House is blessed with Dee and Vern Taylor, Tom Taylor, and Rik Lawrence as its congenial innkeepers. In the spirit of genuine hospitality, they are sensitive to the needs of their guests and by keeping the inn small, they care for each of these needs. This inn, therefore, is both a refuge for seekers of solitude, as well as just the place to discover new and wonderful friends.

THE CARRIAGE HOUSE, 1322 Catalina St., Laguna Beach, CA 92651; (714) 494-8945; Dee and Vernon Taylor, Rik Lawrence, and Tom Taylor, Innkeepers. A New Orleans-style inn with interior courtyard and 6 suites. Four with 2 bedrooms and 2 with one bedroom. Five with kitchens. All have private baths with tub and shower. Rates: $55 to $85, including Continental breakfast. Winter rate, less 15%, Sept. 15 to May 15. Children welcome, no charge. Well-behaved pets welcome. No credit cards accepted. Open all year. Grill available for cookouts. Inn is two blocks from Pacific Ocean for deep sea fishing or swimming. Lawn bowling or tennis nearby.

DIRECTIONS: From Los Angeles, I-5 south to Laguna Freeway which feeds onto Pacific Coast Hwy. (main street of town). Drive 12 blocks to Cress St., turn left. Inn on 2nd corner.

The warmth of rich patterns and objets d'arts in the Primrose Lane guest suite.

EILER'S INN

Laguna Beach　　　　　　　　　　　　　　　　　　　　**SOUTH COAST**

Danish breakfast in the California sun

Homespun ease and good taste in the entry rooms.

Sophistication, simplicity, and comfort in equal parts make Eiler's Inn a classic. From the street the cobalt-blue facade, its bank of French windows topped by graceful fanlights and dressed with lace curtains, is genteel and unassuming. Entering the lobby and adjoining library-game room, the feeling is one of ease, with contemporary overstuffed, bisque-colored couches, a wonderful blonde-wood fireplace which was designed around antique corbels, and baskets of shells and flowers. Walking past these entry rooms one enters an enclosed courtyard, an oasis filled with the combined sounds of a bubbling fountain and quiet classical music. Wrought iron chairs and tables invite guests to enjoy a cool glass of iced tea and a bit of conversation. Overlooking this tropical garden is a two-story gallery of simple, individual, and very comfortable guest rooms which combine antiques and twentieth-century period pieces.

The inn is named after Eiler Larsen, the legendary and colorful Dane, who, in years past, welcomed visitors to his adopted village. It seems quite fitting, therefore, that Jonna Iversen, a transplanted Dane who shares innkeeping duties with Kay Trepp, carry on the Danish tradition of hospitality. Her vivacious personality, combining an infectious smile with boundless energy, makes her one of the inn's greatest assets. Annette and Henk Wirtz, who moved to Laguna Beach from Germany in 1981, round out the inn's complement of genial European hosts.

Breakfast is special at Eiler's. Kay is a superb cook who creates elaborate streudels and coffee rings that

Left: Breakfast buffet in the garden patio.

defy the most stout-hearted dieter. Giant shells filled with an artful melange of fresh fruits are placed on each garden table, while a basket of hard-boiled eggs, a pitcher of fresh squeezed juice, and piping hot herbal teas and Viennese coffee open sleepy eyes and entice guests to linger. Just a few steps from the Pacific, and blessed with a private sundeck with a view of the sea, Eiler's Inn is a gem.

EILER'S INN, 741 South Coast Highway, Laguna Beach, CA 92651; (714) 494-3004; Kay Trepp and Jonna Iversen, Innkeepers. Eleven comfortable guest rooms and 1 suite provide accommodation at this inn. All have private baths with showers, 5 have decks, and there is a choice of double, twin, king, or queen-size beds. Rates, including breakfast: $75 to $125 double; less $5 for single; plus $10 each extra person. Open all year. Children discouraged. No pets. Visa, MasterCard accepted. Numerous restaurants in the area. Close to beach, golf, and tennis.

DIRECTIONS: From Los Angeles, take I-5 south to Rte. 133 and go west to Rte. 1 (Coast Hwy.). Turn left on Rte. 1. Inn is just past intersection of Cleo St. and Hwy.

Leisure deluxe in a lush setting

The flourishing forty-foot-high eucalyptus trees that give the Inn at Rancho Santa Fe its luxuriant, jungle-like setting are the result of a gigantic miscalculation by the Atcheson, Topeka and Santa Fe Railroad. The company wanted to ensure a constant supply of railroad ties for their rapidly expanding operations and, in 1906, planted three million hardy seedlings from Australia on part of the huge sandy tract they owned in Southern California. They found out in due course that it was impossible to cut a flat tie from the twisted trunk of the eucalyptus, so their fine idea was abandoned. They turned the unplanted acreage into a citrus farm, with a part set aside for residential development.

The first structure, built of adobe in California mission-style, was used by the railroad to accommodate prospective land buyers. In 1941, it was bought, along with twenty acres, and turned into a quiet resort where guests could enjoy a little peace in the California sunshine. Mary Pickford was a guest in the early days, and the eminent judge Harold Medina stayed here while doing a Greek translation. Over the years, twenty cottages have been built, and it is now a self-contained community where guests can enjoy leisurely seclusion amid verdant acacia, avocado, palm, and, of course, eucalyptus trees.

The inn has been owned and managed by members of the Stephen W. Royce family since 1958, and the cottages, joined to the main building by walkways and gardens, are simply and comfortably furnished, western-style. Many have sliding doors leading to their own patios, and the mission-style architecture has been retained throughout the complex. The Royce family's collections of antique ship models and oriental treasures lend color and distinction to the main lounge, a huge room with a fireplace and a high, raftered ceiling. Two of the four charming dining areas are the book-lined Library Room and the breakfast room overlooking the swimming pool and patio with umbrellaed tables.

The inn maintains its own beach cottage at Del Mar and will gladly pack picnic lunches. There is tennis on the property, and golfing arrangements can be made at any of three nearby courses.

Dan Royce runs the inn on a very friendly and personal basis. One night a guest appeared at dinner coatless, and on the spot Dan loaned him his own. The guest didn't need the shirt off Dan's back, but he probably could have had that, too.

The cottages are named after flowers. This is Honeysuckle.

Left: The main lounge, with the family's collection of models of antique sailing ships. OVERLEAF: *Left,* a private patio attached to one of the cottages. *Right,* eucalyptus trees abound throughout the twenty lush acres of grounds.

THE INN AT RANCHO SANTA FE, P.O. Box 869, Rancho Santa Fe, CA 92067; (714) 756-1131; Dan D. Royce, Innkeeper. An 80-room inn, with deluxe accommodations in private cottages with baths. Open all year. Rates $40 to $125 double or single; $10 extra for additional guest. Cottages $125 to $250. Restaurant serves breakfast, lunch, and dinner. Children welcome. Visa, MasterCard, American Express, Diners Club accepted. Swimming pool, tennis courts, putting green, ping pong, badminton, and horseshoe pitching. Private beach house for day use at Del Mar, 5 miles from inn.

DIRECTIONS: From I-5, exit at Solana Beach, Lomos Santa Fe. Drive east 4½ miles to inn on right.

Nothing short of spectacular

Built in 1887 for prominent attorney Eugene Britt, Britt House is a beautiful Queen Anne-style structure that has the distinction of being San Diego's first and only bed and breakfast inn.

Before taking the plunge into innkeeping, Daun Martin and designer-husband Robert Hostick first traveled through California visiting established inns, closely observing each in order to discern what did and did not work. They decided, for example, to avoid serving too-sweet breakfast breads, and they also recognized the charm and wisdom of providing wicker baskets in which to tote toiletries to bathroom and sauna. Back home, they combined the best of what they found with their own sense of style and created a truly gracious hostelry.

Left: The imposing entrance hall and staircase.

Each evening Daun prepares a yeast bread which is served in hot loaves at breakfast, along with a soft-boiled egg, fresh ground coffee, freshly squeezed orange juice, a crock of sweet butter, and a pot of jam. A plate of warm-from-the-oven cookies, fresh fruit, and several morsels of chocolate are also delivered daily to each room. On Sunday, Robert prepares a special fruit salad garnished with a wickedly rich whipped cream concoction.

Robert took great pains in decorating the house, and it is a beautiful showcase for his talents. Harking back to the Victorian era, he used a richly hued palette to create a unique personality for each room. King Ludvig, which is the largest guest room in the house, complete with a petite private balcony, is awash in shades of gold, melon, orange, and pink.

Details of the complex wood construction of the inn, which is also shown on the front cover.

The king-size bed's ornate headboard and brocade couch were once furnishings in mad King Ludvig's royal palace. Just down the hall, Ibis is done up in a romantic blend of soft peach, rose, lavender, tan, and gold, and it is simply elegant. Rose-colored glass panes set into bay windows cast warm light across the queen-size brass bed, exquisite Eastlake dresser, and Victorian loveseat.

The inn's entrance hall is nothing short of spectacular. One's eye is drawn immediately to the monumental, two-story stained-glass window depicting Morning, Afternoon, and Evening. Its rich colors cast about like jewels, lighting the imposing yet graceful golden-oak staircase.

To quote a recent guest, the Britt House is, "a lovely retreat from a hectic world—everything we had hoped for, and more."

OVERLEAF: Innkeeper Daun Martin with her husband, Robert Hostick, flanked by two of their staff.

BRITT HOUSE, 406 Maple St., San Diego, CA 92103; (714) 234-2926; Daun Martin, Innkeeper. This mansion has 8 guest rooms in the house and 1 cottage on the grounds. Cottage has private bath and full kitchen. Guest rooms in house share 4 baths, 1 with 2 tubs and 1 with sauna and shower. Rates, including breakfast: $60 to $90 per room. Open all year. Children not encouraged, except in cottage. No pets. Visa, MasterCard accepted. San Diego Zoo is 2 blocks away. Jogging and bicycling in park.

DIRECTIONS: Take Airport-Sassafrass turnoff coming south on I-5. Proceed on Kittner. Turn left on Laurel; left on Third; right on Nutmeg; right on Fourth St., and come down 1 block to the corner of Fourth and Maple.

The imposing stairway, showing stained-glass windows, and *right*, a detail of one.

Innkeepers

Innkeeping in the Far West is part of a tradition that is older than the nation. In 1769, the Franciscan monks who came to California from Spain began to forge a chain of missions along the Pacific coast from what is now San Diego up to Sonoma. The journey north took some twenty-one days, and it was essential that, at the end of each day, travelers be certain of food and shelter. Later, in the wake of men like Jedediah Smith, trappers and mountain men found way stations and trading posts that would take them in. No part of America has a richer heritage of hospitality than the West where, two hundred years ago, a safe refuge could mean the difference between life and death.

Innkeeping today is a quixotic calling; people are drawn to it for any number of reasons. There is the natural satisfaction that comes from extending hospitality to the traveler, but there is also an additional imperative—the challenge of creating a unique and ideal environment. The innkeepers pictured here are just a few of the many who await your pleasure throughout California.

San Ysidro Ranch:
Jim Lavenson

Sutter Creek Inn:
Jane Way

Union Hotel:
Dick and
Teri Langdon

Victorian Farmhouse: Tom Szilasi

Sonoma Hotel:
Dorene Musilli

St. Orres:
Leif Benson
Eric Black
Rosemary Campiformio
Richard Wasserman
Ted Black

SAN FRANCISCO WINE COUNTRY GOLD COUNTRY

Burgundy House:
Mary and Bob Keenan

MENDOCINO

UKIAH

101

Clear
Lake

COAST RANGES

128

Wine Country

LAKE
BERRYES

CALISTOGA INN
WINEWAY   ● **CALISTOGA**
LARKMEAD

WINE COUNTRY INN   ● **ST. HELENA**
CHALET BERNENSIS   CINNAMON
                       BEAR

                    MAGNOLIA HOTEL
● **SANTA ROSA**   **YOUNTVILLE**
                    BURGUNDY HOU
                    WEBBER PLACE

12

SONOMA   YESTERHOUSE
SONOMA HOTEL   ● **NAPA**
CHALET   BEAZLEY HO

116

101   80   680

                    EAST BROTHER LIGHT STA

                    THE FRENCH
                    GRAMMAS BE
                    AND BREAKFA

1   **SAUSALITO** ●**BERKELEY**
    CASA MADRONA   ● **Oakland**

San Francisco
BED AND BREAKFAST INN
HERMITAGE HOUSE   SAN FRANCISCO BAY
WASHINGTON SQUARE INN
INN AT UNION SQUARE
SPRECKELS MANSION
OBRERO HOTEL   *San*
UNION STREET INN
                                 Francisco

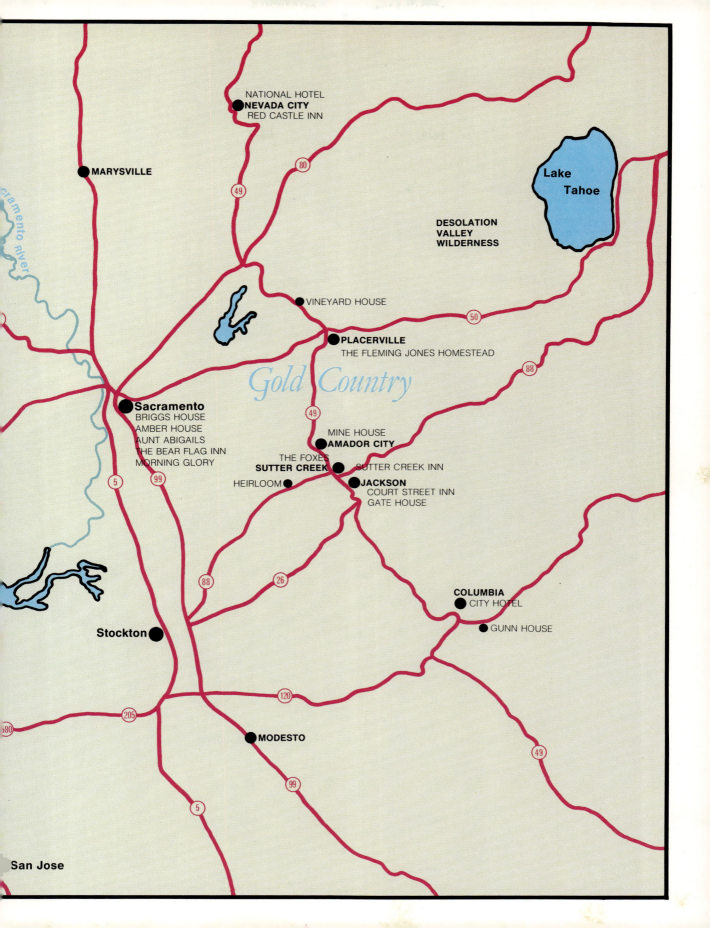

NATIONAL HOTEL
NEVADA CITY
RED CASTLE INN

MARYSVILLE

Lake
Tahoe

**DESOLATION
VALLEY
WILDERNESS**

VINEYARD HOUSE

PLACERVILLE
THE FLEMING JONES HOMESTEAD

Gold Country

Sacramento
BRIGGS HOUSE
AMBER HOUSE
AUNT ABIGAILS
THE BEAR FLAG INN
MORNING GLORY

MINE HOUSE
AMADOR CITY

THE FOXES
SUTTER CREEK   SUTTER CREEK INN

HEIRLOOM   **JACKSON**
                  COURT STREET INN
                  GATE HOUSE

COLUMBIA
    CITY HOTEL

GUNN HOUSE

Stockton

MODESTO

San Jose

Charlton Court BED AND BREAKFAST INN SAN FRANCISCO

A country hideaway in the heart of the city

The rooms are all different and all beautiful.

A country inn is sometimes as much a matter of style as it is of location. Compared to the usual run of impersonal city hotels, the Bed and Breakfast Inn in San Francisco seems like a Napa Valley hideaway. It is a tiny place on Charlton Court, just off Union Street, with only seven rooms and the best San Francisco has to offer.

Innkeepers Bob and Marily Kavanaugh are transplanted from Southern California, and every detail shows that running the Bed and Breakfast Inn is a labor of love for them. The front door is practically enveloped in foliage, and there are fresh flowers in the common room and the guest rooms, as well. Three rooms open onto a lovely garden's profusion of colorful flowers, and one secluded spot is a peaceful, monochromatic Japanese garden. Some of the rooms have such evocative names as Kensington Garden, Green Park, and Willows. Autumn Sun is subdued and restful. The charming frame building next door contains three mini-suites, each with its own distinctive character and each more spectacular than the last. Sydney Greenstreet would approve of The Mandalay, with lots of rattan, a chair with a peacock fan back, a ceiling fan, and mosquito netting over the large comfortable bed. Covent Gardens sports a latticework arcade framing a riot of flowers, and Celebration has a sunken tub.

The Kavanaughs recently moved across the street. Consequently their very special penthouse, The Mayfair Flat, with its spiral staircase to a bedroom loft with king-size bed and double-size tub, is now a favorite accommodation.

English prints are hung in the common room, and the best china is used for a leisurely breakfast of coffee, juice, buttery croissants, and jam. A flower-bedecked tray will be brought to guests who want breakfast in bed, and if Champagne is required for special occasion, it comes in a silver bucket.

For the Kavanaughs, keeping everything shining and blooming is more than a full-time job, but the satisfactions are "incredible," according to Marily. Pinned on her bulletin board in the kitchen is a quote from actress Ruth Gordon: "Never give up, and never, under any circumstances, no matter what, ever face the facts."

The flower-fringed life at the Bed and Breakfast Inn proves that some fantasies make it in the real world.

Breakfast can be had in the common room, *above,* in bed, or on the terrace.

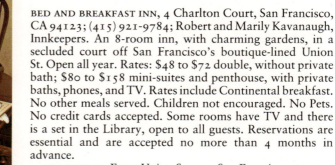

BED AND BREAKFAST INN, 4 Charlton Court, San Francisco, CA 94123; (415) 921-9784; Robert and Marily Kavanaugh, Innkeepers. An 8-room inn, with charming gardens, in a secluded court off San Francisco's boutique-lined Union St. Open all year. Rates: $48 to $72 double, without private bath; $80 to $158 mini-suites and penthouse, with private baths, phones, and TV. Rates include Continental breakfast. No other meals served. Children not encouraged. No Pets. No credit cards accepted. Some rooms have TV and there is a set in the Library, open to all guests. Reservations are essential and are accepted no more than 4 months in advance.

DIRECTIONS: From Union Square, San Francisco, go west on Sutter St. to Franklin St. Turn right on Franklin and proceed to Union St. Turn left on Union to Charlton Court, on left-hand side of Union between Laguna and Buchanan.

Sacramento St.   # HERMITAGE HOUSE   **SAN FRANCISCO**

A magnificent survivor of the San Francisco earthquake

The Hermitage House is the brainchild of Marian and Ted Binkley, who vacationed in European bed and breakfast inns and got the urge to relive those precious moments here in America. Putting themselves in the hosts' position they wanted to share the unique beauty of San Francisco and to meet all of the interesting people who frequent inns. So when they found the perfect seventeen-room, Greek Revival mansion in Pacific Heights, they created one of the loveliest of California's inns.

Before they could open the doors they had the awesome job of restoring the house to its original glory. Built between 1900 and 1903 for Judge Charles Slack, it was given its first renovation after the great San Francisco earthquake. As a point of history, Judge Slack's law books, which he kept in his fourth-floor study, were miraculously preserved from destruction and were the only existing set in the devastated city. The home remained a single family dwelling until the early 1970s, when it became a drug rehabilitation center. Five years later the Binkleys owned the house, and, through a united family effort of scrubbing, oiling, painting, and sewing, they opened their inn in 1979.

Marian Binkley's sense of design and color make the Hermitage House a warm and restful place to stay. Using floral and chintz fabrics and wallpapers, she combines country charm with city sophistication to perfection. One of the most spectacular rooms in the house is Judge Slack's Study, that same room from which the law books were saved. It boasts

The guest rooms are all fabulous, as shown *above* and *overleaf.*

original redwood shakes on the walls as well as the gabled ceiling. With its wraparound bookcases, working fireplace, bay window with inset writing desk, and king-size bed with lots of beautiful pillows, the room is a haven from the cares of the world. The Master Bedroom, decorated with cream and oyster rugs and upholstered easy chairs, and accented by soft, leaf green, is so filled with light that it cheers the gloomiest day.

Because the Hermitage House caters to guests who stay for one week or more, it offers the use of a fully-equipped kitchen on the first floor. Complimentary breakfast is also served downstairs amid the spectacular redwood columns, beams, mantles, and scroll-work that distinguish the first floor.

HERMITAGE HOUSE, 2224 Sacramento St., San Francisco, CA 94115; (415) 921-5515; Marian Binkley, owner. This Greek Revival mansion offers warm hospitality to guests in 10 bedrooms, 8 with baths, 2 sharing. Half have working fireplaces. Queen, king, and twin beds are available. Rates, including Continental breakfast: $40 to $60 single; $40 to $90 double; $10 for extra person. No other meals served; however, guests have kitchen privileges for a larger breakfast or other light food preparation. Long stays given first preference; 5 days or longer, special rates. Private phones. Open all year. Sun deck for guests.

DIRECTIONS: On Sacramento Street between Buchanan and Laguna. Public parking 2 blocks away; unloading zone in front of inn.

WASHINGTON SQUARE INN
INN AT UNION SQUARE

Stockton St.

Post Street

SAN FRANCISCO

Tradition and luxury in two sophisticated inns

How do you start a country inn if you can't bear to leave the city? Nan Rosenblatt solved that problem in 1978 when she bought a building in a charming ethnic neighborhood in San Francisco. There, in the old Italian section off Washington Square, she established a traditional country inn, not far from Coit Tower and Ghirardelli Square. Being an interior decorator, she cheerfully set off for Europe, shopping for country French antiques to furnish the Washington Square Inn. Norman, her husband, a realtor, gave up his other involvements to manage the fifteen-room inn.

Two years later, on Norman's birthday, the Rosenblatts expanded. This time they created a small elegant inn from a vacated hotel that housed troops during World War II. Directly above John Howell's Rare Book Shop, The Inn at Union Square is totally in keeping with the sophisticated neighborhood, where the legendary I. Magnin and St. Francis Hotel are located.

Nan furnished the inn's twenty-seven rooms in period English Georgian, making sure that no two rooms were alike. Meeting lobbies, each with their own fireplace, are situated on every floor for relaxing and taking breakfast and refreshments. Complimentary shoe shines and terry cloth robes are unexpected luxuries.

There are four small suites at The Inn at Union Square and one large one. The latter has a living room with fireplace, TV, stereo, wet bar, powder room, bedroom with a king-size canopied bed, and a bath featuring jacuzzi and sauna. In this suite and others, local art that is on display can be bought. Occasionally guests buy a piece of furniture, which the innkeepers replace.

Both The Inn at Union Square and the Washington Square Inn serve fresh croissants and fresh ground coffee for breakfast. In addition there is English tea, cucumber sandwiches, and short bread, served in the afternoon between four and six, and hot hors d'oeuvres between six and eight, all included in the rates.

Left: Inn at Union Square guest room.

Coit Tower, overlooking Washington Square.

THE WASHINGTON SQUARE INN, 1660 Stockton St., San Francisco, CA 94133; (415) 981-4220; Norman and Nan Rosenblatt, Innkeepers. This uniquely-located inn has 15 guest rooms with private or shared baths and twin, queen, or king-size beds. Rates, including Continental breakfast served in room or lobby: $50 to $105 single; $60 to $115 double; $10 for additional occupant. Tea available every afternoon from 3:30 to 6. Wine and beer available by the bottle. Many fine restaurants in the area. Parking available 1 block away at prevailing charge. Picnics will be packed if requested previous day. No children. No pets. Visa, MasterCard, American Express accepted. All rooms have telephones. Open all year.

DIRECTIONS: Inn is located at corner of Stockton and Filbert Streets opposite Washington Square in Telegraph Hill area.

THE INN AT UNION SQUARE, 440 Post St., San Francisco, CA 94102; (415) 397-3510; Norman and Nan Rosenblatt, Innkeepers. This elegant small hotel, in the heart of San Francisco, has 27 guest rooms, all with private baths and telephones. Paging device available. Twin, queen, and king-size beds. Four small suites, 1 penthouse suite with whirlpool bath, sauna, fireplace, and refrigerator. Rates, including Continental breakfast: $70 to $250 single; $85 to $265 double; $15 for additional occupant. Small lobby on each floor has fireplace, comfortable seating, refrigerator, and glasses. Tea available there afternoons from 4 to 6 and hors d'oeuvres from 6 to 8. Wine, liquor, and beer available by full bottle. Valet garage service available 7 A.M. to 10 p.m.. Children welcome. No pets. Visa, MasterCard, American Express accepted.

DIRECTIONS: Inn located ½ block from Union Square.

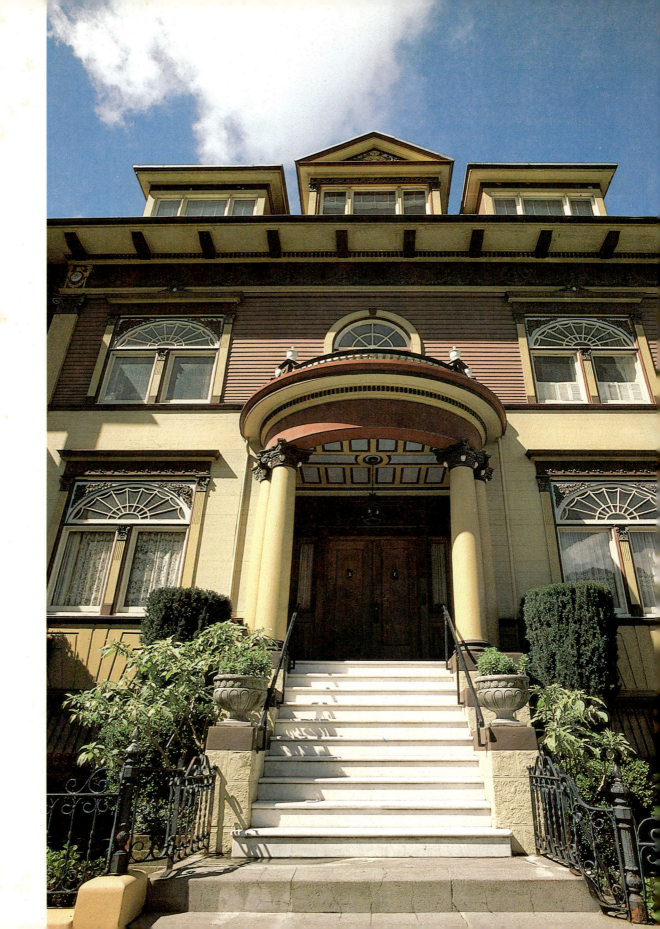

Buena Vista West **SPRECKELS MANSION** SAN FRANCISCO

The ultimate
bed and breakfast inn

Spreckels Mansion, San Francisco's ultimate bed and breakfast inn, traces its origin to the heyday of the Western Sugar Refinery and the famous Spreckels family. Requiring the mansion to have a beneficent location as well as grand and graceful proportions, Richard Spreckels chose, in 1887, to situate his home directly across from Buena Vista Park, a verdant isle of emerald green, high enough atop a hill to afford a breathtaking view of the city.

When Jonathan Shannon, who designs women's evening wear, and his partner, Jeffrey Ross, an architectural restorer, discovered that the mansion was scheduled to be demolished in order to make way for contemporary condos, they were so dismayed they decided to buy the building and convert it into several apartments. But after spending some time within the mansion's walls they realized it was meant to house a single family. What to do? Open an inn, of course!

"We had never been to an inn in the United States but had been to dozens in Europe. So we decided there must be at least five people in the country who would want to stay in this house," laughs Jonathan. It takes but one look at the finely appointed guest rooms to realize there might be five people in the country who *wouldn't* want to stay in the Spreckels Mansion. Just one guest room, for example, is the spectacular Sugar Baron Suite, with its blue-and-cream ceramic fireplace, queen-size bed flanked by Corinthian columns and canopied with gauzy streamers, and clawfoot tub in front of a second open hearth.

When the house next door, which was home to a famous rock musician, came up for sale, Jonathan and Jeffrey quickly bought it and expanded Spreckels

The Sugar Baron Suite.

Mansion from five rooms to ten. Here you can choose among such comforts as the cozy Gypsy Hideway, with its amber and garnet paisley-draped bed, tapestry pillows, working fireplace, and huge picture window, and the Stargazer Suite, complete with beehive fireplace, a glass-and-shingle shower which is open to the skies, custom designed woodwork, and a skylight over the bed for romantic evenings under the stars.

THE SPRECKELS MANSION, 737 Buena Vista West, San Francisco, CA 94117 (415) 861-3008; Jonathan Shannon and Jeffrey Ross, Innkeepers. The inn comprises a Colonial Revival mansion and a neighboring townhouse with 10 elegant guest units, including 4 suites. All have private baths with showers and most have tubs. Some working fireplaces. Rates, including a Continental breakfast and complimentary wine: $85 to $215, the latter being for the San Francisco Suite covering the entire 3rd floor of the mansion; $10 for each additional person in a room. Each room has either double or queen-size bed and telephone. No children. No pets. No cigars. Two night minimum stay on weekends. Open all year. Breakfast served to rooms in main house. Next door it is left by room door in an English picnic basket.

DIRECTIONS: Buena Vista West is off Haight St., at base of Buena Vista Park. Wind up the hill to 737.

The Stargazer Suite. OVERLEAF: View of University of San Francisco from the inn.

The Garden Room, *above,* and the library, *right.*

OBRERO HOTEL

Stockton St.   SAN FRANCISCO

Originally a haven for Basque shepherds

A biochemist turned world traveler, Bambi McDonald spent eight years living and working in Europe. When she returned to the United States she was very well versed in the economies of European pensions. After holding a series of jobs unrelated to biochemistry, she ended up at the Obrero, a former pension for Basque sheepherders. Beginning first by upgrading the neglected guest rooms, she also took time to observe the kitchen proceedings of the Basque restaurant, which was still operating. By the time the restaurant owners decided to retire, she felt confident she could carry on the Basque dining tradition. And so, seven days a week, Bambi offers a *prix fixe* family-style Basque dinner in her cheerful dining room, its tables decked out in red-and-white checkered cloths and its walls hung with kitchenware.

Breakfast at the Obrero is so substantial that, aided by a mid-afternoon tea, it carries most guests through to dinner. Ham, cheese, a four-minute egg, an orange, hot sourdough bread, San Francisco honey, and your

Left: In the heart of Chinatown, next to a green grocer.

choice of hot beverage are included in the price of the room. Each chamber in this walk-up hotel is furnished with a brass bed and a firm matress, and a puffy comforter covered with cheerful Marimekko fabric livens up the decor. All rooms must share bathrooms down the hall, but the entire hotel can be counted on for simple comfort and cleanliness.

OBRERO HOTEL, 1208 Stockton St., San Francisco, CA 94133; (415) 986-9850; Bambi McDonald, Innkeeper. A refurbished small hotel in San Francisco's Chinatown. There are 12 comfortable rooms, 10 with double beds and 2 with 2 double beds. All share 4 baths but each has a wash basin. Rates, including a full breakfast: $20 single; $27 double; $32.50 for two people in 2-bedded room; $40 for 3 people in room. The hotel is home to a well known Basque restaurant which has been operating for many years. Reasonably priced dinner is served at 6:30 P.M. and reservations are necessary. Wine is included with dinner. The hotel has a wine and beer license. Children welcome. No pets. No credit cards accepted. Open all year. Check-in times, 8 A.M. to noon and 5 to 10 P.M. Closed noon to 5. No smoking in bedrooms. Nine blocks from Union Square. Good public transportation to all San Francisco's famous attractions.

DIRECTIONS: Hotel is between Broadway and Pacific on Stockton St. Public parking available around the corner on Broadway.

Innkeeper Bambi McDonald.

With a flower-filled private garden

The Union Street Inn is a special find for inngoers. Owner Helen Stewart, who spent most of her life teaching art, has created an easy atmosphere of comfort and hospitality. This Edwardian townhouse is comprised of a sitting room with blazing open hearth, apricot velvet wall coverings paired with cream-colored moldings, and a cozy clutter of books, plants, and plush easy chairs. Two bedrooms on the first floor and three upstairs are furnished with a combination of antiques and contemporary pieces, and each is dressed in its own dashing color scheme. Walk through French doors in back to a private garden filled with camellias, lilacs, violets, and a sprightly holly tree. A rustic path leads to the guest cottage Helen recently added. Inside, a sunken jacuzzi-for-two lit by an overhead skylight, lush potted plants, and bamboo furnishings make this cottage a special haven for lovers. Located in one of the city's most energetic neighborhoods, the inn is central to a top-notch selection of restaurants and shops.

UNION STREET INN, 2229 Union St., San Francisco, CA 94123; (415) 346-0424; Helen Stewart, Innkeeper. A handsome Edwardian home, now a 5-room inn with beautiful garden cottage. Of the aptly named rooms, New Yorker and English Garden have queen-size beds and private baths; Golden Gate, Holly, and Wildrose, with queen, king or long twins, double bed respectively, share 2 baths. All have wash basins in attractive alcoves. Carriage House has jacuzzi tub, small refrigerator, and attractive bay window. Rates, including Continental breakfast: $64 to $94 in the house; Carriage House $135 double; $15 for each extra person. Breakfast may be served in rooms, parlor, garden, or deck. No other meals served but an abundance of excellent restaurants within walking distance. Open all year. Children over 12 welcome; otherwise by special arrangement. No pets. Visa, MasterCard, American Express accepted. Frequent bus service on Union St. brings all the city's points of interest within easy access.

DIRECTIONS: From north or south on US 101, west on Union St. to Fillmore St. and 2200 block. Public parking nearby.

A brilliant mix of antique and contemporary.

THE FRENCH HOTEL

Modern elegance in a changing neighborhood

At the same time that boutiques and specialty food shops were changing the character of North Berkeley, the elegant French Hotel emerged. The old brick building, formerly a laundry, received an additional floor. Rooms with luxurious contemporary furnishings feature dramatic lighting and dusty rose, grey, and robin's-egg-blue silk hangings and quilts. Newly constructed private decks and patios provide views of San Francisco and the Berkeley hills, and there is a French cafe in the lobby serving pastry and coffee.

Directly across the street is Chez Panisse, one of the restaurants that has made Berkeley the gourmet sensation of the Bay area. Started by Alice Waters, Berkeley '67, the restaurant offers fresh king salmon, calvados soufflé with carmelized apple slices, and stuffed cabbage and artichokes.

Marilyn Rinzler's Poulet is two blocks away. Marilyn, Berkeley '75, is the chicken-jewelry-wearing proprietor of a delicatessen and restaurant that is devoted to serving chicken in every conceivable form.

Narsai's, whose proprietor is one of the area's leading restaurateurs, is also nearby. Through great, special dinners, big-hearted Narsai supports community causes! KQED public TV benefitted from a recreation of Prince Charles and Lady Di's wedding feast, and another fabulous fund-raising dinner helped finance East Brother Light Station.

THE FRENCH HOTEL, 1538 Shattuck Ave., Berkeley, CA 94704; (415) 548-9930; Phil Pezzuto, General Manager. An elegant, small urban hotel situated in North Berkeley. Seventeen rooms with private baths; 14 of the rooms have private patios or decks. Open all year. Rates: $58 to $75, double; 2 suites $85, including Continental breakfast. Cafe open 7 days from 7 A.M. to 10 P.M. Children welcome. No pets. TV and phone in each room. Reservations requested. Visa, MasterCard, American Express accepted. A choice of excellent restaurants in immediate vicinity. A small collection of specialty shops nearby. Seven blocks from University of California.

DIRECTIONS: From I-80 take University Ave. exit, continue to Shattuck and turn left, hotel in 6th block.

Modern European elegance.

A fine old house with decorative plaster ceilings that could never be duplicated today.

"Come home" to a superb bed and breakfast inn

A visit to Gramma's Bed and Breakfast Inn feels akin to a visit with your own grandmother, or perhaps it's the way we all wish it could be. Enter this stately turn-of-the-century Tudor home, past lush flowers and a pair of illuminated goslings, to discover an inviting living room. It beckons. Sink into one of the overstuffed velveteen couches or comfortable easy chairs and browse through the good selection of magazines, or read a newspaper left by a previous occupant. Glancing about the room you'll notice the ornate plaster friezes that band the ceiling, the detailed inlaid hardwood floor, and Victorian lamps, their velvet shades casting an amber glow. The sharpsighted will note a basket of peanuts next to a neighboring chair and the crock of buttery shortbread on the sideboard. Sigh with pleasure and sink deeper into your chair. You've come home.

To find your room you'll climb the stairs and pass by a giant-size photograph of Elizabeth Taber, the woman to whom the inn is dedicated. Gramma's owner, Kathy Lustig, has wonderful memories of her grandmother, who ran a boarding house in Boston. Continue up to your room, which might be a tiny nook with a cushioned windowseat, an armoire, and an antique bedstead, or one of the larger rooms with a reading chair or a large private deck overlooking the garden.

From this vantage point you can see the renovated garden cottage that houses eight guest rooms. All of the rooms in the cottage have working fireplaces and most have decks flanking their entrances. Throughout, the inn's mood is light and comfortable, a mood that's achieved, in part, by dainty country prints and handmade quilts, but which is created mostly by the congenial people who work at the inn.

Breakfast is served each morning in the sun room at the back of the main house or on the adjacent redwood deck. During the week fresh fruits and breads are the featured fare, while on weekends quiche and bagels with lox and cream cheese are offered as well.

GRAMMA'S BED AND BREAKFAST INN, 2740 Telegraph Ave., Berkeley, CA 94705; (415) 549-2145; Kathy Lustig, Innkeeper. An English Tudor-style house in the heart of Berkeley with 19 guest rooms, 11 in the main house and 8 in the garden cottage, all with private baths. Open all year. Rates, including Continental breakfast: $65 to $95 double; $15 for extra person. Set charge for extra guests at breakfast. No other meals served. However, a variety of outstanding dining establishments are available in Berkeley. No children under 6. No pets. All major credit cards accepted.

DIRECTIONS: From I-80 take Ashby Ave. exit into Berkeley. Continue on Ashby Ave. to Telegraph Ave., turn left on Telegraph to Ward and left to inn parking lot.

CASA MADRONA

Sausalito   SAN FRANCISCO

Continental elegance in an opulent mansion

A spectacular view.

In 1885, William Barrett, a transplanted Vermonter who had made a fortune in lumbering, built his dream house on one of the hillsides of Sausalito. It was an Italianate Victorian pile, with marble fireplaces, stained-glass windows, and extensive iron grillwork, set in an impressive terraced garden overlooking San Francisco Bay. Barrett's villa became the showplace of a community of gracious homes.

As is often the case with fine old nineteenth-century houses, Casa Madrona went somewhat to seed after its original owners departed. For a while it was used as a hotel, an inn, and, if local rumor is correct, even as a bordello. During the 1950s, it became a community crash pad for members of the beatnik generation. Restoration of the old place was begun in the 1960s by Robert Henri Deschamps, a restaurateur with a fine sense of Continental elegance. He leased the hotel and installed Le Vivoir, a French restaurant of such excellence that San Franciscans, who know something of fine cuisine, immediately declared it one of the premier establishments in the Bay Area. Le Vivoir has since moved to another location on the north coast, and in its place are 16 new cottages, stair-stepped up the hillside.

John Mays, an attorney with the eye of an artist, discovered the Casa Madrona in 1976, bought the establishment, and set about restoring the upstairs rooms to their original grandeur.

The result is a splendid California hotel with the warmth and style of a European country inn. Each of the accommodations, including a separate guest house, is a creation with its own name and personality. The Gingham Room is delightfully Victorian in cheery blue and white, while the Mariner Room features nautical touches in a sturdy setting of natural redwood and brick. The Fireside Room still has the original mahogany fireplace and a sweeping view of the harbor, while the Regency offers an impressive king-size canopied brass bed. Guests may be reminded of Casa Madrona's giddier days in the Bordello Room.

Left: All the rooms are restored to their original charm, with comfortable additions.

But whichever room they select, guests will find that, after almost one hundred years, the Casa Madrona is once again what it started out to be—a dream house.

CASA MADRONA HOTEL, 156 Bulkley Ave., Sausalito, CA 94965; (415) 332-0502; John W. Mays, Innkeeper. A magnificently restored 1885 mansion overlooking yacht harbor. Fourteen rooms, all but 4 with private baths, and 5 cottages each accommodating 4 persons. Rooms have double, king, or queen-size beds. Rollaway bed available for additional guest in room. Open all year. Rates, including Continental breakfast in sitting room, from $45 to $95; cottages $110 to $115. All cottages have operating fireplaces. Wine with cheese and crackers served in sitting room. Restaurants in nearby downtown Sausalito. Children welcome. Pets allowed in cottages. Visa, MasterCard, American Express accepted. Interesting browsing in nearby art galleries and craft shops.

DIRECTIONS: A ½-hour ferry ride across the bay from San Francisco; by car, take US 101 over Golden Gate Bridge. Take first exit after bridge (Alexander Ave.) to downtown Sausalito. At first traffic light turn left on Princess St. Bear right up hill on Bulkley Ave. to hotel on right-hand side.

PHOTOGRAPHED BY DENNIS DUGGAN

EAST BROTHER LIGHT STATION

Point Richmond

SAN FRANCISCO

A unique country inn

Beyond realizing the fantasy of staying in a lighthouse, a stop-over at East Brother Light Station ensures the continued success of a non-profit corporation. In 1979 three hundred local volunteers and a grant from the Department of the Interior restored the station that was slated for demolition.

From Point San Pablo's Yacht Harbor it is a fifteen minute boat ride to East Brother Island's pier. The Victorian buildings on the island have been totally restored and its guest quarters furnished with period pieces. A tradition of self-sufficiency remains intact. Wood-burning stoves for heating, a cistern for collecting water, and solar collections for heating water are all part of that effort.

Pat Jackson, the keeper of the light station, was one of the volunteers who helped restore it, and she now manages the inn. Pat conducts tours and is partly responsible for the surprising dinners. Chicken Kiev, Caesar salad, and poached pears Anglaise are served in this "living museum," dedicated to the niceties of country-inn dining.

For people looking for someplace different to stay, this working light station more than fills the bill.

EAST BROTHER LIGHT STATION, 17 Park Place, Point Richmond, CA 94801; (415) 233-2385; Pat Jackson, Lightkeeper; Walter Fanning, Volunteer Assistant Lightkeeper. The inn is a Victorian carpenter Gothic house on East Brother Island in San Pablo Bay. Open Thursday through Sunday. Two rooms in the house and one in a cottage have double, queen, and king-size beds. One ½ bath and 1 full bath in house. Rates, including dinner and breakfast: double occupancy Thursday and Sunday $145 per night; Friday $155 and Saturday $175. Varied rates for extra persons. Rate includes transportation by boat from Point San Pablo Yacht Harbor. Enquire about day use Friday, Saturday, or Sunday. Children are welcome for day-use activities but must be under supervision of parent at all times. Children may accompany overnight visitors only with specific permission of keepers. Wines and aperitifs are available for over-night visitors and are served at meals. No pets and no smoking allowed inside any building. Phone or send for brochure for further information.

DIRECTIONS: As visiting the Light Station is by reservation only, explicit directions will be given when reservation is made.

The restored dining room.

With three acres of Sonoma countryside

Lolita Murphy always collected things, so when her kids grew up and it was time to turn her home into an inn, she already had all the items that add warmth and color to comfortable period furniture. Bright silk coverlets and log-cabin-patterned quilts hang on the walls, two on either side of a china closet, whose shelves are arranged with a collection of dolls. There are old books of short stories and intriguing mysteries, and a collection of lace doilies and dresser scarves distinguished by figures worked into their intricate patterns. California pottery from the forties in pastel shades of blue, lavender, rose, and green brighten up the kitchen, and are used for serving guests country-fresh scrambled eggs laid by the Murphy's chickens.

On the grounds behind the house is the barn the Murphys have converted into their living quarters. The previous owner held dances there, and you can still see the Swiss murals his brother painted in several rooms of the Chalet. All of the guest rooms here have balconies or decks from which to enjoy the country setting.

If you do venture off the balcony and the Chalet's three acres, there are famous wineries to visit in Sonoma. For those guests who like flea markets as much as the Murphys do, there are some nearby in Sausalito, Sebastopol, and Alameda, open on weekends the year round.

CHALET, 18935 - 5th St. W., Sonoma, CA 95476; (707) 996-0190 or 938-3129; Patrick and Lolita Murphy, Innkeepers. A farmhouse on 3 acres offers guests 4 rooms with private or shared baths, double or twin beds, and balconies. Rates, including full breakfast served at breakfast table or outside: $50 double; $15 for each extra adult or $5 to $10 for extra child. Open all year. Each floor has small refrigerator and stove for cold or hot drinks. Sherry or wine in each room. Children over 5 accepted during week. Small dogs accepted. No credit cards accepted. Within walking distance of historical sites and 1 winery. Bicycle paths. Hot tub on the grounds.

DIRECTIONS: From Sonoma town plaza take Spain St. to 5th and turn right. At end of road is sign "Chalet."

The dining room, showing the colorful pottery collection.

Victorian elegance, western style

Sonoma county lays claim to being the "cradle of California history," and Russian, English, Mexican, Spanish, and American flags have flown over the region at various times. The northernmost mission in Alta California, then under Mexican control, was built here in 1823 and was the site for the town of Sonoma, founded several years later.

The hotel was probably built somewhere around 1872, but it was used for various purposes before becoming a hotel in 1920. The present-day innkeepers, John and Dorene Musilli, bought it in 1974 and set about restoring the hotel to a proper nineteenth-century hostelry, refurnished with authentic items from the days of the Barbary Coast and the Gay Nineties. The building, with adobe infill, was structurally sound; but inside, the banisters and trim had to be laboriously stripped of eight layers of paint to get down to the wood. The two etched-glass panels in the double front doors give a proper Western touch to the entrance, and the main sitting room is a warm gathering place looking out on the town square. The hotel has seventeen distinctive guest rooms. Room 3 is furnished with a rosewood bedroom suite, on loan from the Sonoma League for Historic Preservation, that once belonged to an illustrious resident of Sonoma, General Vallejo, the governor of Alta California. Room 2 offers a five-piece suite made of hand-carved wood and rare orange marble, and another guest room contains a suite of solid oak inlaid with ebony. There are several fine brass bedsteads, and Room 29 features an enchanting pair of hand-carved Austrian children's beds, a French dresser with its original tin mirror, and a graceful chandelier.

The adobe relics of early Sonoma are everywhere around the town plaza. The old mission is located on one corner, and on the north side is the Mexican Soldiers' Barracks and the restored but nonfunctioning Hotel Toscano. Down the street is the Blue Wing Inn, built by General Vallejo in 1840 and now made over into antiques shops. The Blue Wing's guest book shows visits from such Wild West personalities as John C. Frémont, Kit Carson, and the bandit Joaquin Murietta.

Left: An exotic brass bed dominates room 1.

The lobby, set for breakfast of croissants and coffee.

Sonoma also lays claim to another very important event in California history. A young Hungarian nobleman, Agoston Haraszthy, had spent ten years searching the new continent for soil comparable to that in his homeland suitable for viniculture, and he finally found what he was looking for in Sonoma. In 1855, he bought 500 acres just east of town, which he planted with cuttings from Europe. With this first planting, the California wine industry was born.

SONOMA HOTEL, 110 West Spain St., Sonoma, CA 95476; (707) 996-2996; John and Dorene Musilli, Innkeepers. A 17-room hotel in a historic town in the wine country. Private and shared baths. Open all year. Rates $35 to $55 double; $32.50 to $55 single; including Continental breakfast. Rooms in rear are quietest. The inn now operates the restaurant with the addition of a beautifully restored 120-year-old bar from Harlem. Lunch and dinner are served on the rear patio in good weather. Children welcome. No pets. Visa, MasterCard, American Express accepted. Sightseeing in historic town; visits to local wineries.

DIRECTIONS: From San Francisco, take US 101 to Rte. 37 at Vallejo. Turn off Rte. 37 onto Rte. 121 to Sonoma. Hotel is on northwest corner of the town plaza.

Solar energy.

Sunlight filters through the lobby curtains. The etched-glass design on the front door, below right, lends a western feeling. The historic district adjacent to the plaza is a very pleasant place to stroll.

A special combination of enthusiasm and dedication

The Beazley House, a 1902 Colonial Revival, weathered-shingle mansion is one of Napa's architectural masterpieces. Enter through an original stained glass door into a spacious foyer dominated by a grandfather clock and softly colored oriental-style rug. Just to the left, the spacious living room with its small-paned windows, inlaid oak floors, fine mahogany wainscoting, and cushioned windowseat, is especially attractive. Bedrooms range in size, from a large suite with fireplace and beautiful brass-and-porcelain bedstead to a small sunporch overlooking treetops and the lush backyard. Breakfast is served downstairs in the sunny formal dining room, and the abundance of fresh fruits, cheeses, and hot muffins is very satisfying.

But the greatest reward for staying at the Beazley House is meeting Carol and Jim Beazley. They love the Napa valley and are particularly proud of the town of Napa, which is experiencing a renaissance. The Beazleys recognized this fact early on and opened the first bed and breakfast in the city. Today, their united enthusiasm and dedication make this inn a very special spot.

BEAZLEY HOUSE, 1910 First St., Napa, CA 94558; (707) 257-1649; Carol and Jim Beazley, Innkeepers. An inn with 6 guest rooms sharing 3 baths, 1 with shower only, 2 with tub and shower. Accommodations in a carriage house include 4 suites with private baths and fireplaces. Rates: $65 to $85 double; $15 for extra person; includes a generous Continental breakfast. Sherry available on sideboard. Menus from local restaurants available; assistance with reservations offered. Children under 12 not encouraged. No pets. No smoking. Visa, MasterCard accepted but checks preferred. Two-night stay required on weekend. Especially interesting: bicycle riding and architectural walking tours of Napa.

DIRECTIONS: From Rte. 29 take 1st St. (central Napa) exit. Take 2nd St. exit off ramp and go 3/10 mile and turn left on Warren. Inn on corner of 1st and Warren.

One of the prettiest brass beds we've seen.

Napa

YESTERHOUSE INN

WINE COUNTRY

A sweetheart of an inn

For anyone who enjoys fine antiques or just beautiful things done up like a romantic valentine, the Yesterhouse Inn is sheer delight. Innkeeper Paula Weir has spent her life collecting treasures, and finally, through innkeeping, she's found a way to share them. Paula's awesome collection, which is predominantly turn-of-the-century, ranges from a beadwork and needlepoint gout stool, a marble hand commemorating Queen Victoria's coronation, and a vitrine filled with fine art glass in the formal rooms, to an authentic Hoosier pie cabinet and an old fashioned green enamel stove in the kitchen.

The inn offers rooms in the main house, including the campy Uncle Ben's Room, decorated in red, white, and blue, with a quilt of the 46 states, circa 1915; armed forces' sweetheart pillows; photographs of all the family members who served; and a cane rocker with flag afghan. Grandma and Grandpa Card's Room has a carved walnut bedroom set, pie crust tilt-top bird-cage table, framed fans, quilts, and a sitting alcove set off by ruffled organdy curtains.

If your style leans more toward the contemporary, Paula offers two cottages next door whose style is strictly twentieth century—1920s to be exact.

YESTERHOUSE INN, 643 Third Ave., Napa, CA 94599; (707) 257-0550; Paula Weir, Innkeeper. The inn, a Victorian home in the town of Napa, offers 8 guest rooms, 4 in the house and 4 in cottages. Private and shared baths. Rates, including Continental breakfast and complimentary wine: $55 to $95 per room. Children not encouraged. No pets. Smoking discouraged in house. Open all year. Visa, MasterCard accepted. Croquet, frisbee, and board games. Antiques-interest group meetings. All Napa Valley attractions to be enjoyed.

DIRECTIONS: From Rte. 29 take 1st St. (Central Napa) exit. Note: do not take Napa/Lake Berryessa exit. Take 3rd St. exit off ramp and go approximately 1 mile to inn.

A charming, warm inn full of Victoriana, such as this album.

Antiques, picnics, and neighboring vineyards

Built in 1884 by John Thoman, a prominent wine maker, Chalet Bernensis is located next to a working winery in the heart of Napa Valley. Surrounded by spacious grounds, this lovely wide-porched Victorian house has been carefully restored—complete with a replica of its original tank tower—by innkeepers Jack and Essie Doty.

First opened as an antique shop by the Dotys in 1975, the inn overflows with choice early-American and Victorian furnishings. Ornate brass or iron bedsteads, colorful handmade quilts, and lacy curtains enliven five upstairs bedrooms, sharing showers and claw-foot tubs. In addition, four guest rooms in the neighboring tank tower have fireplaces, private baths, and air conditioning.

A Continental breakfast of homemade bran muffins or scones and fruity, homemade jams is laid out in the comfortable sitting room overlooking the garden.

Guests can browse the inn's antiques shop, picnic on its grounds, or enjoy coffee or sherry on the wide, shaded porch.

A new museum in St. Helena displays mementos of Robert Louis Stevenson, and Calistoga Mineral Hot Springs is near by. For more active guests wanting to enjoy the full scenic beauty of the Napa Valley, there is gliding, biking, and hot-air ballooning.

CHALET BERNENSIS, 225 St. Helena Hwy., St. Helena, CA 94574; (707) 963-4423; Jack and Essie Doty, Innkeepers. The spacious old Victorian home was built in 1884 in this small town in the Napa Valley wine country. Five guest rooms, with shared baths. Four additional rooms, with private baths and fireplaces, in the Tank House. Rates: $45 to $50 double, in the inn, and $65 in the Tank House, including Continental breakfast, the only meal served. No children under 12. No pets. No smoking is requested. Open all year. Reservations at least 2 weeks in advance. Visa, MasterCard accepted. Within walking distance or a short drive are a number of wineries, for touring and wine tasting.

DIRECTIONS: From Vallejo, take Rte. 29 north. Inn is just south of the town limits of St. Helena.

A spacious Victorian home built in 1884.

Taste and style in a classic mold

A canopied extravaganza.

Stone terraces lead downhill from this charming country inn to a patio edged with olive trees. A series of balconies offers sweeping views of the valley and the hills beyond. Chinese pistachios grow along the driveway, and even in January daisies bloom by the outside stair. The stone tower, the distinctive roof lines, the walls of board and batten are reminiscent of Continental Europe and have a definite flavor of the style of building in the early days in the Napa Valley. The settlers who came over in the second half of the nineteenth century, many of whom helped start the California vineyards, would feel very comfortable here. The Wine Country Inn looks as if it had long been part of the landscape, and it is a surprise to learn it was only built in 1975.

Ned and Marge Smith had always wanted to be innkeepers, and for years they spent their vacations at inns in the British Isles, New England, and the West, gathering ideas for their own inn. When they were at last ready to build, they went to an artist, instead of an architect, who sketched their inn exactly the way they wanted it. Then they designed the rooms to conform to the overall plan, purposely giving each one a significant feature of its own, such as a balcony or a patio or even a fireplace. The result is an inn with all the character and style of the nineteenth century combined with the sophisticated comforts of the twentieth.

The common room is a large, brightly-lit area paneled in barn siding, with comfortable sofas and chairs, an iron stove, and a long English harvest table where breakfast is served. The Smiths were active in the interior decoration, too, and Marge made many of the lovely quilts for the handsome guest rooms. All have been distinctively decorated, one in red, white, and blue, another with twin headboards made of wine-cask bases. The Smiths thoughtfully widened a Victorian headboard so it could accommodate a king-size mattress.

Left: The driveway up to the inn is lined with oaks.
OVERLEAF: Napa Valley in January. *A view of the inn building appears on page 1.*

A leisurely breakfast is the only meal served at the inn, but there are a number of fine restaurants in the area. A selection of their menus is kept on the table in the common room for guests to look through, and the Smiths will make the reservations. Guests are invited to keep their wines in the inn's refrigerator, and a cupboard in the common room is kept well stocked with glasses.

It is this kind of personal attention to detail that contributes to the rich heritage of hospitality in a country inn. Ned and Marge Smith are already innkeepers in the classic mold.

WINE COUNTRY INN, 1152 Lodi Lane, St. Helena, CA 94574; (707) 963-7077; Ned and Marge Smith and Jim Smith, Innkeepers. A stunning 25-room inn built in the style of early Napa Valley buildings. Private baths. Open all year. Rates: $70 to $100 double; single $3 less. Rates include buffet-style Continental breakfast, the only meal served. Children over 12 welcome. No pets. Visa, MasterCard accepted. Nearby wineries open to visitors.
DIRECTIONS: Rte. 29 through Napa Valley. North of St. Helena, 2 miles, turn at sign for Lodi Lane. Inn's entrance just down the road on left.

CINNAMON BEAR

Makes you feel like you never left home

Born and raised in St. Helena, Genny Jenkins recognized that the town lacked comfortable accommodations for visitors to her spectacular native valley. So when her children flew the nest she converted the substantial home they had shared into a warm and charming bed and breakfast inn. Because she's kept the furnishings pretty much the way the family left them, her inn has a feeling of genuine, homey comfort. Not fond of refurbished antiques that end up looking like slick reproductions, Genny's collection of antique furnishings show their years in both form and finish. Every bedroom has a private bathroom, stocked with lovely soaps, bath salts, a rubber duck, and plush towels. The mood in each room is so genuine it makes you feel like you never left home.

The name "Cinnamon Bear" was born when some of her first guests began to brainstorm for an appro-

priate moniker. Genny's collection of stuffed bears, which began with gifts from her son, a bear aficionado, caught their fancy. Today, dozens of stuffed bears and spicy bear candies can be found in corners, on cupboards—in fact, just about everywhere!

CINNAMON BEAR, 1407 Kearny St., St. Helena, CA 94574; (707) 963-4653; Genny Jenkins, Innkeeper. Each of the 4 guest rooms has private bath, 1 with shower, 3 with tubs only. Rates, with lavish Continental breakfast: $66 double; less $5 for single person; add $10 for 3rd person. Open all year. No children under 8. No pets. No credit cards accepted. No smoking in bedrooms. No smoking in common rooms if other guests object. Port and wine available in parlor. Cheese and crackers in the afternoon. Good restaurants in area. Museum of Robert L. Stevenson memorabilia.

DIRECTIONS: From Napa take Rte. 29 to St. Helena. At Adams turn left, drive 2 blocks to corner of Adams and Kearny. Inn is on corner.

A cuddly welcome from "Teddy" in each guest room.

LARKMEAD

Genteel warmth
in vineyard country

"People who stay here can't resist going out among the vines and 'rubbing elbows' with the grapes," laughs Joan Garbarino, owner and innkeeper of the Larkmead Country Inn. Given the inn's idyllic location, in the midst of vineyards, the temptation seems quite natural.

Noted not only for its perfect setting, the inn is an architectural gem as well. Solid yet elegant, this Italianate home was built in 1918 by the owner of the Larkmead Vineyards. In order to enjoy the surrounding fields he built a long covered veranda that looks out upon large sycamore trees, which shade a rustic stone fence. In the garden, hybrid roses nod languidly while fragrant jasmine and wisteria climb trellises; dwarf orange trees and colorful geraniums line the gallery and fill window boxes.

Inside, guest rooms are comfortable and lovely, but the living room is magnetic. Its soft dove grey walls are filled with books, and its broad fireplace crackles cheerfully on cool days. Fine Persian rugs, classic upholstered and antique wooden furniture, and a fine collection of prints and paintings resonate genteel warmth.

At breakfast the emphasis is on quality, starting off with Joan's special blend of fresh-ground coffee and fresh fruit, and ending with wonderful hot cross buns, muffins, or flaky pastries. Thus fortified, the pleasures of the Napa Valley—from wine tasting to hot mud baths—gently unfold.

LARKMEAD COUNTRY INN, 1103 Larkmead Lane, Calistoga, CA 94515, (707) 942-5360; Joan and Gene Garbarino, Innkeepers. Completely surrounded by 4 vineyards. Open 11 months, closed January. Four guest rooms with private baths; 1 with shower and tub, 3 with showers only. Rates: double $75; 10% less for single; $20 for extra guests over 2; includes Continental breakfast. No other meals served. Complimentary decanter of wine each evening. Children under 16 not encouraged. No pets. No credit cards. In town are a number of spas offering mud baths, hot springs, and massage. Wine tours in the area, as well as ballooning, bicycling, soaring, or hiking.

DIRECTIONS: From the south take Rte. 29N. Larkmead Lane is 4.5 miles north of St. Helena. Turn right, inn is on right side of road.

The inviting living room is the focus of the inn.

On the western slope of the Napa Valley

Together, Dede and Allen Good wanted to put a lot of effort into something they could do successfully. At their Wine Way Inn they do just that. Anxious to get started, they bought a house that needed little fixing. The western slope of the Napa Valley comes down to their property line, and they were delighted to learn they owned part of a mountain.

Running the inn is very much of a cooperative effort—making up rooms, gardening, and baking the raspberry and cinnamon coffeecakes they serve for breakfast. They take a personal interest in guests, and make reservations at spas in Calistoga and at small wineries, as soon as they know when guests are arriving.

Guests will find the house quaint but not luxurious. The living room has shoulder-height fir paneling, a beamed ceiling, fireplace, and nineteenth century American furniture. At the far end, the dining room has a leaded-glass breakfront that displays a dazzling collection of pewter, silver, china, and crystal.

When Dede was pregnant, guests took quite an interest. They kept track of the due date, and called to check on her; after the baby was born, some sent gifts. Baby is now part of the team, and the song ought to go:

"Just Alan and Dede and baby makes three—
They're happy at Wine Way Inn."

WINE WAY INN, 1019 Foothill Blvd., Hwy. 29, Calistoga, CA 94515; (707) 942-0680; Dede and Allen Good, Innkeepers. This 1915 farmhouse is now a comfortable inn offering 6 guest rooms; five in the house and 1 in a guest cottage. Private and shared baths. Double, queen, and twin beds. Rates, including a Continental breakfast served in the dining room: $60 to $75 double; single rates on request. Closed December and January. Children over 10 welcome. No pets. Visa, MasterCard accepted. Relax on the beautifully located redwood deck, or in sitting room by fireplace if weather dictates. Innkeepers will assist with dinner reservations or arrange winery tours. Calistoga is noted for its therapeutic mineral springs and spas.

DIRECTIONS: Rte. 29 to Calistoga. Inn on Rte 29, which becomes Foothill Blvd. On the left 1 block before turning into center of town. Fence in front with white gravelled parking area.

Great Food but modest rooms

Calistoga, at the terminus of the Napa Valley, is famous for the mineral springs which spawn healthful bottled waters and soothing mud baths, for celestial soaring at the downtown airstrip, and, of course, for vineyards. Located on the main street of this variegated village, the Calistoga Inn is known to most people simply as a fine restaurant, and that it truly is. Owner Philip Rogers tailored the inn after hostels he found while traveling in provincial France, and he is doubly blessed with the husband-and-wife team of Frank Coffey and Audrey Holman, who bring to the table generous portions of such toothsome culinary delights as delicate fried calamari or an Oregon blue cheese mousse appetizer. Dinner might include mar-inated-and-grilled sturgeon en brochette with sesame sauce or braised duck in caper-sage sauce, with an apricot vacherin with kiwis and strawberries Chantilly or a poached pear with creme a l'Anglaise and chocolate sauce for dessert. The added bonus at this inn are the eleven guest rooms upstairs, noteworthy not for their charm, for they have none, but for the fact that they offer travelers a share in this beautiful area at a very reasonable cost.

CALISTOGA INN, 1250 Lincoln Ave., Calistoga, CA 94515; (707) 942-4101; Philip Rogers, owner. Eleven rooms with wash basins. Two women's baths, 1 with shower, 1 half bath. One men's bath with shower. All double beds. Rates, including Continental breakfast: $25 single; $30 double. Excellent restaurant serves dinner daily except Monday. Full bar. Children and pets not encouraged. Visa, MasterCard accepted. Open all year.

DIRECTIONS: Rte. 29 to Calistoga. Inn is on main street just next to Napa River.

Yountville # WEBBER PLACE **WINE COUNTRY**

An innkeeper who loves restoring things his way

For Loren Holte there are no rules for things, so when he bought the old Webber place, he restored it his way. Built in 1850, the farmhouse had no studs or sheet rock, so Holte took it apart and rebuilt it from the inside. Along with architect Ray Rector and carpenter Mike Johnson, he pulled down tongue-and-groove ceilings and put in new rafters and joists. Because the redwood and fir had been painted, he took it down and reversed it to restore the natural wood. There was no accounting for his plumbing feats either, but his handiwork is a joy to behold. In two of the guest rooms large porcelain tubs have been set on raised tile floors.

In the treatment of guests, there are no hard and fast rules either. It is not unusual for a husband to get up early and fix his wife's breakfast, nor was it odd when one of the guests put on an apron and

Left: One of the guest rooms, showing the glorious, natural redwood.

served the other guests breakfast. Once a French family staying at the inn decided to cook dinner and, after gaining "kitchen privileges," they prepared a gourmet meal complete with vintage wine and expensive cigars. Although Holte does not encourage guests cooking at the inn, he believes if you respect people, they won't disappoint you.

Cooking is the last thing you have to do when you stay at the Webber Place. The town of Yountville has three thousand people and fifteen restaurants, of which three, the French Laundry, the Magnolia Hotel and Domaine Chandon, are among Northern California's finest.

WEBBER PLACE, 6610 Webber St., P.O. Box 2873, Yountville, CA 94599; (707) 944-8384; Loren Holte, Innkeeper. Open all year. Four guest rooms, private and shared baths, in an 1850s restored farmhouse. Rates, including Continental breakfast: $55 to $90 double; $15 for 3rd person. Children over 16 welcome. No pets. Visa, MasterCard accepted. Guests greeted with a glass of wine and offers of information on local attractions, special events, or best places to dine. Open all year.

DIRECTIONS: Take I-80 to Vallejo or Napa exit, then Rte. 29 to Yountville. Inn is at corner of Webber and Jefferson streets.

Romantic and secluded; luxurious and indulgent

The playfully decorated lobby.

Bruce Locken, innkeeper at the Magnolia Hotel, has spent most of his life making guests comfortable in such places as the Casa Munras in Monterey and the Clift Hotel in San Francisco, where he was once general manager. Despite his high-powered background, Bruce has found his true happiness running the Magnolia Hotel, a small, seven-room establishment in Yountville. As Bruce explains, it is a case of "Why didn't we do this before?" The "we" includes Bonnie, who is Magnolia's chef and Bruce's wife, along with two sons and a daughter-in-law.

The Napa Valley is becoming an increasingly popular tourist attraction, and people come in growing numbers each year to see the vineyards and taste the wines. A good deal of the valley's appeal, however, has to do with the charm of such places as the Magnolia Hotel. Bonnie particularly cherishes a cookbook inscribed by Julia Child, giving her enthusiastic approval of the meal she enjoyed at the Magnolia.

The bright red lampshade draped with tulle in the lobby may make guests think, at first, that they've stepped into a scene from *East of Eden,* but the abrupt little stairway leads to seven stylish guest rooms above, each with a private bath. "Everything we do is first class," says Bruce proudly. And everything is, from the marble-topped vanities to the magnolia-scented soap and sumptuously comfortable beds.

The smallest, most private room is on the third floor. "It's a favorite with couples on a second honeymoon," says Bonnie. A large bed fills practically all the space, and the window behind it has a view of the town. "When people stay up here," she says, "we find they seldom leave their room." When they do, it is probably for the splendid breakfast served at the large table in the dining room downstairs, where guests are treated to delicious French toast with a port wine syrup, one of Bonnie's creations.

Dinner at the Magnolia is served in an adjacent brick annex that the Lockens have decorated with great care. Chairs of white oak are placed at tables draped with lace cloths and set with the finest china and silver. Bonnie cooks a different meal each evening, usually featuring a classic French dish. Occasionally, she makes an exquisite chicken paprika, or a Viennese roast loin of pork.

The redwood deck behind the inn is a perfect place to relax and enjoy a soothing whirlpool spa in fenced-in privacy. The Locken's Siamese cats wander about with a proprietary air, and the all-pervasive mood of the Magnolia Hotel is at once romantic, secluded, luxurious, and indulgent.

MAGNOLIA HOTEL, 6529 Yount St., Yountville, CA 94599; (707) 944-2056; Bruce and Bonnie Locken, Innkeepers. A 7-room hotel, dating from 1873, in the Napa Valley wine country. Private baths. Open all year. Rates: $60 to $125 double, including complete breakfast. Complimentary decanter of wine in each room. Restaurant serves lavish 5-course dinner Friday and Saturday by reservation only. Extensive wine cellar features more than 300 varieties of California wine. No children under 16. No pets. No credit cards accepted. Swimming pool and heated jacuzzi. Boutiques, art galleries, wineries, and balloon rides nearby.

DIRECTIONS: From Rte. 29, take Yountville exit, drive north on Washington St., which continues into Yount St. Hotel is on the left.

The elegant brick dining room in the annex.

Yountville | # BURGUNDY HOUSE | WINE COUNTRY

A tub for two and vineyards in view

In 1870, Charles Rouvegneau came to Yountville, a sleepy little village settled in the 1830s, and built a small, sturdy fieldstone house similar to the ones in his native France. Rouvegneau made wine on the first floor and rented out the rooms upstairs. Over the years, the building was used for many things, not all of them respectable, and in 1975, Mary Keenan, a local antiques dealer, and her architect husband, Bob, took the place over for a shop. By then, the house had acquired a hundred years' worth of stucco, paint, and plaster. Bob had everything sandblasted down to the original stone and wood, inside and out. When Mary opened her store, so many customers wanted to stay there that she was inspired to convert it into an inn. But Burgundy House is still an antiques shop, too, and guests have the unexpected pleasure of being able to live with something before actually buying it.

The Keenans are Francophiles, and French country antiques predominate. Their colorful personal touches include needlepoint Mary brought from Hong Kong, a chess set, and other antique games plus a glorious cupboard hand-painted by a San Francisco artist. An upstairs bath has an antique shaving mirror, plants, an oversized tub with gold-painted claw feet, and a park bench for visiting. No clocks are to be found in the inn, as the Keenans feel that their guests shouldn't have to worry about time.

There is always a fire in the long common room in the winter, and in the summer the guests take their breakfast, the only meal served, out onto the secluded patio and enjoy the view across the Napa Valley vineyards to Mount Veeder in the distance. The guest rooms are bright and cheerful, with flower paintings hung on the stone walls. Some have elaborately carved Victorian bedsteads, others antique iron or brass, set off with ruffled pillows, richly patterned comforters, or silken sheets. Each guest room has its own decanter of Napa Valley wine, and there is always a selection of sherry, Burgundy, and zinfandel for the guests in the common room. The accommodations have been expanded by a splendidly spacious suite in a store the Keenans remodeled across the street, and by a

OVERLEAF: A colorful cupboard in one of the guest rooms, and the famous tub-for-two.

Napa Valley vineyards from the common room.

tiny house decorated in rich browns and reds.

An additional building down the street, Bordeaux House, has now been added, and is furnished in a more contemporary style. Breakfast is served at Burgundy House.

The increasing interest in the Napa Valley vineyards has spawned several fine restaurants in the area, and champagne flights in a hot-air balloon from a nearby field offer a unique means of seeing the Napa Valley.

BURGUNDY HOUSE COUNTRY INN, 6711 Washington St., Yountville, CA 94599; (707) 944-2855; Mary and Bob Keenan, Innkeepers. A 12-room inn in a Napa Valley wine-country town. Six rooms in inn share baths; 6 rooms in 3 cottages with private baths. Open all year. Rates: $40 to $99 double, including Continental breakfast and wine. No dining room but list of recommended restaurants in area available. Children allowed in cottages. No pets. No credit cards accepted. Swimming pool, mineral baths, Champagne balloon rides within 8 to 10 miles.

BORDEAUX HOUSE, rates $40 to $115, including a Continental breakfast served at Burgundy House.

DIRECTIONS: From Rte. 29 take Yountville exit, drive north through town on Washington St. to inn.

Five inns with
a common purpose

What was an uninteresting coffee stop on a traveler's itinerary is becoming a destination: Sacramento. The seat of California's government, its completely restored capitol building reflects the pride of this vast state. A new railroad museum, the Crocker Art Museum, and Old Sacramento, which is a renovated nineteenth-century shopping area along the riverfront, are attracting crowds.

As a result of this renaissance, five bed and breakfast inns have opened their doors, run by like-minded individuals. These innkeepers banded together to offer each visitor better and more complete service. Today, the Amber House, Aunt Abigail's, The Bear Flag Inn, Briggs House, and Morning Glory inns represent the Sacramento Innkeeper's Association. Though each has its own unique style, they all conform to high standards set by the group as a whole.

AMBER HOUSE is the essence of tailored elegance. Everything is polished to a gleaming finish. The innkeepers offer quiet surroundings and special amenities for the business traveler amid a rich atmosphere of fine, antique furnishings.

AUNT ABIGAIL'S is one of Sacramento's architectural gems, reminiscent of the city in its heyday. The first floor is grand and spacious, the living room opening onto Mary Lou Rienecker's colorful garden. The inn is decorated with pieces she collected while in India, as well as a variety of family memorabilia and mixed period pieces.

THE BEAR FLAG is a family affair. Besides raising their own family in the inn, the Wests welcome travelers with children. Decorated in fine gothic revival style, with William Morris design chairs and wallpaper, the inn ranks high for warmth and comfort.

Left and above: The Briggs House, outside and in.

BRIGGS HOUSE, which was the first bed and breakfast to open in the city, is elegantly appointed with fine antiques and good reproduction furniture. But, above all, this inn is comfortable. The largest of Sacramento's inns, with five bedrooms in the main house and a two-bedroom suite in the restored backyard cottage, the Briggs House offers such amenities as breakfast in bed and a relaxing jacuzzi and spa.

MORNING GLORY, which is a 1906 Colonial Revival bungalow with lovely beveled and leaded-glass windows, is also geared toward families. Innkeeper Joy Reed is a caterer as well as innkeeper who does right by her guests, serving a variety of homemade delights, from apple walnut waffles with genuine maple syrup to her special quiches.

AMBER HOUSE, 1315 - 22nd St., Sacramento, CA 95816; (916) 444-8085; Bill McOmber and Robert O'Neil, Innkeepers. This attractive inn, recognizable by its handsome brass nameplate, has 4 guest rooms, private and shared baths, double beds. Rates: $62.50 to $75 double; rollaways available at additional cost. Continental breakfast served in room. Decanter of California sherry available in library for guests. No children. No pets. Visa, MasterCard, American Express accepted. Seven blocks from Capitol building and downtown. Complimentary pick-up service at downtown airport limousine terminals and local train stations. Convenient off-street parking. Bicycles may be borrowed. Open all year.

AUNT ABIGAIL'S, 2120 G St., Sacramento, CA 95816; (916) 441-5007; M. L. Rienecker, Innkeeper. This turn-of-the-century Colonial Revival inn has 5 guest rooms, private and shared baths, and double, twin, or king-size beds. Rates, including Continental breakfast: $45 to $55 single or double; $10 for 3rd adult or $5 for a child. Children and pets welcome. Visa, MasterCard accepted. Space for meetings, conferences, parties, or weddings. Attractive court yard and garden opening from living room. Open all year.

Amber House.

The Bear Flag.

THE BEAR FLAG INN 2814 I St., Sacramento, CA 95816; (916) 448-5417; Robert Henry West, Innkeeper. A California-Arts-and-Crafts-style bungalow offers 2 guest rooms with double beds and private baths. Rates: $40 single or double, includes Continental breakfast with grapefruit from the garden served in the kitchen or garden. Children welcome. Pets welcome. No credit cards accepted. Two blocks from Sutter's Fort and within walking distance of several fine restaurants. Open all year.

BRIGGS HOUSE, 2209 Capitol Ave., Sacramento, CA 95815; (916) 441-3214; Bob and Sue Garmston, Barbara Stoltz, Kathy Yeates, and Paula Rawles, Innkeepers. This 1901-vintage house features 5 guest rooms with private and shared baths. A 6th bedroom suite, for 1 or 2 couples, in a secluded carriage house in the garden. Rates, including generous Continental breakfast: $50 to $65 double. Complimentary wine in the evening. Sauna and jacuzzi available. Children not encouraged. No pets. Visa, MasterCard, American Express accepted. Open all year.

MORNING GLORY, 700 - 22nd St., Sacramento, CA 95815; (916) 444-2885; Joy Reed, Innkeeper. A restored 1906 Colonial Revival home offers 4 guest rooms, private and shared baths, and double beds. Cozy flannel sheets in winter and lemonade or iced tea in summer. Rates: $45 to $75 double, including a generous breakfast of homemade specialties, served in kitchen or garden; inquire about single rates; $5 to $7.50 for child, according to age. Children welcome by prior arrangement. No pets. No credit cards. Smoking restricted to porch or garden. Space for receptions, meetings, luncheons, or dinners. Catering provided. Open all year.

DIRECTIONS: Five Sacramento inns are located in an old residential area east of, or in back of, the capitol building and park. The area is bounded on the south and east by highway I-80. East to west streets are lettered alphabetically, and are in a "one way" grid. From San Francisco on I-80, at Sacramento take 15th street exit, drive east 1 block to 16th street, turn left on 16th, go to Capitol ave., turn right on Capitol to 22nd. All the inns are in the immediate area.

OVERLEAF: A Virginia and Truckee Railroad 2-6-0 locomotive strikingly displayed in the new Sacramento Railroad Museum, which is part of a major effort at historical preservation in the city.

Aunt Abigail's.

Centerpiece of a museum town

Two brothers struck gold in 1850 in what turned out to be the heart of the California Mother Lode. Within a month, some six thousand miners were working the area, and by the time they were done, some eighty-seven million dollars worth of gold had been extracted from the Columbia field. As the mining camp grew fron tents to a proper town, the miners felt they needed a little class in their public establishments, and in 1856 the What Cheer House was built. It was rebuilt in 1867 after a fire, along with much of the rest of town, and was renamed the City Hotel in 1874.

In its time, the building has been a newspaper office, the local opera house, and an assay office, but it was as a tavern and hotel that it was best known. Now, as the result of a massive restoration project by the State of California, it is once again in business and is the focal point of the Columbia State Historic Park. The entire community is a working museum of the exciting Gold Rush days, and the town is so well preserved it is often used for filming TV westerns. Many of the miners were homesick easterners who had solid Victorian furniture brought overland by wagon or around Cape Horn by ship. The rooms at the City Hotel would delight them today, and of the nine guest rooms, Room 1 is the star. It has its own balcony door, and the massive carved walnut bedstead is supposed to have belonged to the warden of San Quentin Prison. The rooms have their own half-baths, and guests shower down the hall following the nineteenth-century custom.

The hotel's chef came from Ernie's, one of San Francisco's finest restaurants. The French and international cuisine would flabbergast the old miners, used to beef jerky and chap whiskey, who certainly couldn't have spelled *chateaubriand* and wouldn't have known what it was, anyway.

Left: The dining room, restored to its former glory. OVERLEAF: The building's façade, completely restored. On the following pages are two views of other restorations in Columbia's commercial district: *Left,* the Wells Fargo office, and, *right,* the familiar corner filmed in many westerns.

Gold Rush days brought back to life in the guest rooms.

Thanks to the farsightedness of the State of California, what might have been a ghost town in the Gold Rush Sierra country is very much alive, and the City Hotel is the perfect base for visiting this fascinating area that has seen so much of California's history.

CITY HOTEL, Main Street, Columbia, CA 95310; (209) 532-1479; Tommy Bender, Innkeeper. A 9-room hotel in a re-created Gold Rush town. Private half-baths, with shower down the hall. Open all year except Christmas. Rates $48.50 to $55.50 double, including Continental breakfast. Restaurant, offering fine French cuisine and vintage wines, serves lunch and dinner daily except Mondays. Sunday Brunch 11 A.M. to 2 P.M. all year. Children welcome. No pets. Visa, MasterCard accepted. Hotel is the focal point of a handsomely restored Mother Lode town in Columbia State Historic Park. What Cheer Saloon in hotel; Sierra Railroad nearby.

DIRECTIONS: Three hours' drive from San Francisco, hotel is 3 miles north of Sonora on Rte. 49. Hotel is on Main St., closed to traffic during the day in summer. Take alternate road around town center and park in back of hotel.

A living link with California's fabulous past

The thick-walled, two-story adobe that Dr. Louis Gunn built on Washington Street in 1851 was one of Sonora's few substantial buildings at that time. Serving as Dr. Gunn's home and the office of the local newspaper, the *Sonora Herald,* which he also ran, the building was the focus of political controversy in the 1850s when Dr. Gunn defended the civil rights of Chinese laborers. An outspoken liberal from Philadelphia, Dr. Gunn so angered the local citizenry that they once hauled his printing press onto the street and incinerated it. Dr. Gunn moved to San Francisco in 1861; and as Sonora expanded over the years, so did his old house. Eventually, the original adobe was only one section of a long-balconied building that served for a time as a hospital, then as the city hall, and finally, as a hotel.

Its present good looks are the result of a restoration and expansion undertaken by Mrs. Margaret Dienelt

in the 1960s. The now three-story Gunn House climbs the steep hill on which it is built, and at the back a beautiful stone terrace has been laid out around an oval swimming pool. Whether in the old adobe section, or in one of the newer rooms overlooking the pool, the Gunn House offers an exemplary way of life in this bracing, yet sometimes hot, climate.

An interior courtyard provides the focus for the sprawling complex, and its wrought-iron grillwork recalls the town's early Mexican heritage. Just off the courtyard there is a parlor with a stone floor and extravagant Victorian furnishings, complete with a gilt-framed mirror and a pedal organ in one corner. Much of the decor of the twenty-seven rooms, all with their own baths, is also Victorian, with many walnut and mahogany-mirrored vanities that graze the ceiling.

There's a lively holiday spirit at the Gunn House, since guests are apt to be just starting their vacation or just finishing one. Among the many local sights are the Sierra Railroad, at nearby Jamestown, and several Gold Rush towns. The Gunn House is a living link that gives a new generation of visitors a real feeling of California's fabulous past.

The color-coordinated swimming pool.

Left: A second floor sitting room, restored and elegantly furnished.

GUNN HOUSE, 286 South Washington St., Sonora, CA 95370; (209) 532-3421; Peggy Schoell, Innkeeper. A 27-room inn expanded and restored from an 1850s adobe house. Located in a Gold Rush town in the Sierra foothills. Private baths. Open all year. Rates, including morning coffee and rolls: $36.54 to $66.22 double, depending on sleeping accommodations. No restaurant. Children welcome. Pets accepted at innkeeper's discretion. Visa, MasterCard accepted. Swimming pool. Columbia State Park and Sierra Railroad 3 miles away.

DIRECTIONS: Take Rte. 49 to Sonora. Inn is on right just south of town center on Rte. 108 (South Washington Street).

GATE HOUSE INN

Every amenity, plus a few extras

Innkeeping, for the most part, is extraordinarily demanding work, but after operating the gold country's finest restaurant, the Sutter Creek Palace, Ursel and Frank Walker find it to be a respite. They chose innkeeping as a logical alternative to their breakneck pace as restauranteurs and are bringing to the Gate House Inn, a beautifully maintained turn-of-the-century farmhouse, the same spirit, energy, and perfectionism that made the Palace superior.

Set on the edge of Jackson, adjacent to beautiful farmland, the Gate House has every amenity plus a few extras: a swimming pool, screened barbecue area, and crisp, freshly ironed bed linens! Says Ursel with a smile, "Every innkeeper offers their guests something special. I iron sheets." Attention to detail does

Left: Breakfast at the Gate House is as good as it looks.
OVERLEAF: The Gate House Inn.

not stop here, though. The complimentary morning meal is served on Ursel's lovely English bone china, which she collected during her childhood, and the table is set with antique, crested bronzeware. The open and gracious rooms are highlighted by Frank's collection of fine clocks, and each bedroom is fresh, charming, and impeccably clean. All of this plus an easy and low-key atmosphere make the Gate House Inn a perfect home away from home.

GATE HOUSE INN, 1330 Jackson Gate Road, Jackson, CA 95642; (209) 223-3500; Frank and Ursel Walker, Innkeepers. A country-style Victorian inn offering 5 guest rooms in the house, 1 with ½ bath, 3 sharing, and 1 in the adjoining "Summer House" with full bath and air conditioning. Open all year. Rates, including Continental breakfast: $35 to $60 single; $40 to $65 double (check for possible changes); Monday to Thursday $5 to $10 less. A number of good restaurants, some within walking distance. No children. No pets. No credit cards accepted. Swimming in outdoor pool. Billiard table in game room. Amador County Museum.

DIRECTIONS: From Sacramento, Rte. 50 to Rte. 16 toward Jackson. At Rte. 49 go south through Sutter Creek. Turn on Jackson Gate Road on the left before reaching Jackson. About 1 mile to inn.

Wood, the essential building material in the West, can be beautiful.

An adventure in restoration

Restoring the Court Street Inn was an adventure for Mildred Barns, who bought the Victorian three-story frame house in 1980. In the parlor is a wonderful carved marble fireplace she found behind a bricked wall. Hidden doors to bedrooms appeared, and an obstructed root cellar was uncovered. The newest restoration is the small brick building behind the inn. It was used by the former owner, whose mother ran the Wells Fargo office, as a museum for Indian artifacts. Mildred has restored the tile roof and floors, cedar-lined walls, and fireplace. She uses the "Indian Museum" for serving guests wine and cheese and for selling antiques.

Five years ago, when Mildred was in Singapore and Taiwan, she sent back the oriental pieces that now enrich the house. A black lacquer screen and a

Left: The parlor, with its rediscovered marble fireplace.

carved-ivory chess set are prominently displayed. Combined with Victorian furniture, such as the inlaid burl walnut side-by-side and carved velvet-covered side chairs, the effect is opulent. Old books, her own "Baby Dimples" doll in the dining room, and an old photograph of her family from New Jersey add warm personal touches.

A full gourmet breakfast is served, determined by the whim of the cook. Fruit compote, eggs Benedict, quiche, french toast, flaming crepes, and Champagne are featured. Newlyweds are served on a sunporch off their room, which is always reserved for honeymooners.

COURT STREET INN, 215 Court St., Jackson, CA 95642; (209) 223-0416; Mildred Burns, Innkeeper. The inn, a charming Victorian-style house, has 5 guest rooms with private and shared baths. Rates, including a full breakfast served at 9 A.M.: $35 to $60 double. Open all year. No children. No pets. No credit cards accepted. Two blocks to downtown Jackson. Amador County Museum around the corner. Historic Serbian church and graveyard nearby. Inn is air-conditioned.

DIRECTIONS: Rte. 49 or Rte. 88 to Jackson. Court Street leads directly off the main street in the business section.

Mildred Burns, tending the flower garden in front of her delightful inn.

Southern comfort in the gold country

Patricia Cross and Melisande Hubbs have never advertised their inn. There is no need to. Word of mouth has passed from guest to guest for good reason. Friends for ten years, they have furnished the inn with the contents of both their former homes, after their children grew up and left. Even the china and silverware used for serving a gourmet breakfast belonged to them before they opened their inn.

The furnishings in this ante-bellum southern-style house are conversation pieces. The living room has more than its share of history: the wonderful rosewood piano that is over 150 years old belonged to Lola Montez, and Patricia bought it during the Depression for one hundred dollars. Because it sounds like a clavichord, it's perfect for playing ragtime and Bach. The hand-painted silk, lace, and tortoise shell fans atop the piano belonged to Melisande's French great-great-grandmother, whose picture sits behind them. Brought back by missionaries from China, the hope chest behind the couch belonged to Patricia's mother.

Many of their wonderful possessions were used for Patricia's daughter's wedding in the inn's spacious garden. The guests were impressed, and now many community receptions and social gatherings have become commonplace there.

THE HEIRLOOM, 214 Shakeley, P.O. Box 322, Ione, CA 95640; (209) 274-4468; Melisande Hubbs and Patricia Cross, Innkeepers. The inn, a southern-style house built in 1863, offers 4 guest rooms with private or shared baths. Rates, including a delicious breakfast: $35 to $60. Breakfast served in bed, on the veranda, or in dining area of beautiful main room. No other meals served. Innkeepers will suggest many good dining places in the area. No children. No pets. No credit cards accepted. Open all year. Wine tasting in Amador County wineries. Historic countryside worth exploring.

DIRECTIONS: From Rte. 16 or Rte. 88 take Rte. 124 to Ione. On Shakeley Street watch for "Heirloom" sign on the left. Down a short lane is the inn.

Ante-bellum buildings are rare in the gold country.

One magnificent Victorian suite

The single suite at The Foxes in Sutter Creek offers privacy, luxury, and the complete attention of Pete and Min Fox. From their courtesy airport service, to the rich Victorian furnishings, to the elegant silver breakfast service, the Foxes succeed at making you feel special.

Special, too, is the word for Min's antiques shop. There is a fine selection of French armoires and Chinese embroideries. The rare embroideries are fragments of antique garments employing the "forbidden stitch." This work was so fine it caused blindness and an Empress of China finally forbade her subjects to do it over a century ago. Finally there are the silk flowers Min arranges, and the potpourri she makes from the petals of roses, irises, camellias, chrysanthemums, and other flowers from her beautiful garden.

"Two years ago we said, 'Let's do something with the two extra rooms'," Min says. "We couldn't think of anything nicer to do."

THE FOXES IN SUTTER CREEK, 77 Main St., P.O. Box 159, Sutter Creek, CA 95685; (209) 267-5882; Pete and Min Fox, Innkeepers. One suite in an 1857 New England-style house. Bedroom, sitting room, private bath with shower, and queen-size bed. Rates, including Continental breakfast: $60 Sunday through Thursday; $70 Friday and Saturday. Two day minimum required weekends, Friday–Saturday or Saturday–Sunday. No smoking is requested. No Children. No pets. Visa, MasterCard, American Express accepted. Excellent choice of restaurants in the area. Courtesy airport service (Jackson-Westover Field). Inn is air-conditioned. Open all year.

DIRECTIONS: From San Francisco through Sacramento on I-80 to Rte. 50. Turn on Rte. 16 to Jackson. At Rte. 49 go south to Sutter Creek. Inn is on the right in heart of town.

Sutter Creek # SUTTER CREEK INN **GOLD COUNTRY**

An inn that sets the standards for others

The breakfast room.

Sutter Creek is fifty miles south of the famous spot in the American River where a carpenter discovered gold flakes in the water near the sawmill owned by John Sutter. It is a quiet town with many restored buildings and simple, wooden Gold Rush homes painted blue, red, and yellow. The Sutter Creek Inn was built in 1859 by one of the town's leading merchants for his New Hampshire bride, and it started out as a Greek Revival cottage. The addition of an ell, a front porch, and various outbuildings gave it its own distinctive flair, and it is typical of many homes that grew and expanded to serve the needs of successive owners.

Jane Way chanced on it in 1966 when she was on a trip through the Gold Rush country with her children. It had been empty for some time, and she fell in love with it on sight. There were a few snags, but she bought it and converted it into a country inn. The house is filled with her family's furniture and the results of her own extensive antiquing forays. The living room has two sofas flanking the fireplace with a sled-topped coffee table between, a beautiful big hutch from Boston, and a large chest from Quebec.

Breakfast is a major event, served at nine o'clock sharp in the huge, eat-in kitchen. Jane whacks a big gong, and she and her staff cook up platters of eggs, pancakes, and muffins. If any guests are late, they've lost out, but the aroma of fresh coffee and hot breads usually gets most people up willingly. If anyone is hungry again by lunchtime, or even by dinnertime, Jane provides a list of local restaurants that includes her own capsule reviews.

Jane has expanded the accommodations by converting the old service buildings, each keeping the name of its original function: Upper Washhouse, Cellar Room, Woodshed, and Miner's Cabin. Each house is different, reflecting Jane's wide-ranging tastes, and the grounds are landscaped with walkways, little gardens, and shade trees providing a peaceful retreat. Most unusual at Sutter Creek Inn are the swinging beds which combine a bed with a hammock, an idea Jane got from a friend. They can be made stationary, but most people love the gently rocking motion.

"Once you get used to them," says Jane, "they're much more comfortable than water beds. I'd give them about two nights."

SUTTER CREEK INN, 75 Main St., Sutter Creek, CA 95685; (209) 267-5606; Jane Way, Innkeeper. An 18-room inn in a Gold Rush village. Private and shared baths. Open all year except Jan. Rates $35 to $75 midweek, $50 to $85 weekends, all doubles, including full breakfast for guests only, served at 9 A.M. sharp. Coffee, tea, and brandy served before breakfast. Children over 15 welcome. No cigars, pets, or hair dryers. No credit cards accepted. Croquet, hammocks, swings. Picturesque town, interesting shops, excellent restaurants.

DIRECTIONS: Located 50 miles east of Sacramento on Route 49, 3 miles north of Jackson.

OVERLEAF: *Left,* the inn's Victorian bay window aflame with Pyracanth berries. *Right,* R.W. Tyler, a local gallery owner, has written a *Stroller's Guide to Sutter Creek.*

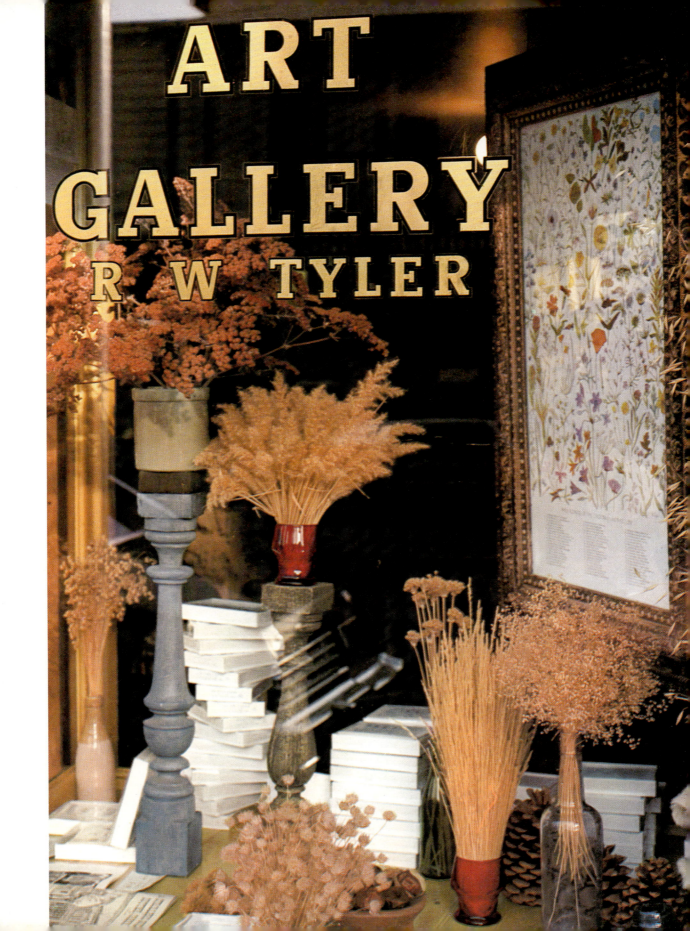

MINE HOUSE INN

Amador City | GOLD COUNTRY

The charmingly converted guest rooms.

A charming inn with Mother Lode connections

The neat, rather elegant brick building, with its white pillared porch, is set on a hill overlooking the tiny Mother Lode settlement of Amador City. It once belonged to the Keystone Consolidated Mine and shares a hillside with the ruins of the original stamping mill. After the mine closed in 1942, the future of the old building was doubtful until the Daubenspeck family bought it in 1948 and converted it into an inn.

"The early owners of the mine had Southern connections," says innkeeper Peter Daubenspeck III, "and the mine offices were pretty obviously designed in a variant of the southern plantation-style." A wide, white-painted board fence climbs the hill to The Mine House, and in spring, daffodils bloom in profusion.

The Daubenspecks have treated what they found with great respect. Most of the private baths have been fitted into what were originally large closets. One room has a shower built into an arched brick structure that supports the vault where the heavy safe that held gold bullion still stands.

Furnishings in the beautifully kept inn are almost all Victorian pieces found locally. As a whimsical tribute to the necessities of yesteryear, a china chamber pot is placed at the foot of each bed. On the walls are engravings and popular art from the late nineteenth century. In the Retort Room, where $23 million in gold was smelted into bullion, a quaintly-framed wall plaque reads, "Charity Never Faileth." The typically Victorian high ceiling of the Director's Room is intact, and sheer curtains give a soft romantic look to the Keystone Room.

The prospect of the town below from the rocking chairs on the front veranda, and the more secluded porch in back adjacent to a sun-screened terrace, with a view up the hill to the magnificent trees and

Left above: The Mine House in its gold-country setting.
Below: the local store, a treasure trove of collectibles.

meadow, would make any guest want to linger. The press of a button in the morning will bring juice and coffee to a guest's bedroom door, and a pool offers a refreshing respite after a day of sightseeing in the Gold Rush country.

Not all the gold is gone. According to the Daubenspecks, the vein was far from exhausted when the mine was closed, but the cost of getting it out now would be prohibitive. All the same, it's nice to think of gold hiding there under the hill, a reminder of the prosperous past.

THE MINE HOUSE INN, Amador City, CA 95601; (209) 267-5900; Peter Daubenspeck III, Innkeeper. An 8-room inn in a former mine headquarters building in a tiny gold town. Private baths. Open all year. Rates: $37 to $44 double; $33 to $39 single, including breakfast, fruit juice, and coffee, tea, or hot chocolate for children. Extra person: child $2, adult $4. No restaurant. Children welcome. No pets. No credit cards accepted. Swimming pool. Antiques and craft shops, wine tasting room in town; restaurants nearby.

DIRECTIONS: On Rte. 49, 2 miles north of Sutter Creek.

FLEMING JONES HOMESTEAD

A country farm with free-running chickens

Back when Placerville was still a wild and wooly mining town, Fleming Jones owned part interest in a local gambling saloon. He also had a wife named Florence who worried constantly that her old home was going to go up in flames. So one night, when Fleming plunked $1200 in winnings in front of Florence with the order to build herself a new house, she did. Several generations later the Fleming Jones Homestead is a down-home country inn complete with free-running chickens, a Welsh pony, and two twenty-year-old donkeys. Janice Condit is the owner and moving spirit behind this irresistable inn. She's rejuvenated the house and barns and filled the place with antiques, bric-a-brac, lots of reading material, and comfortable beds. Surrounded by wooded acreage, the Homestead is pefect for hikes and picnics—or

Left: For the nostalgic, the Good Old Days brought back to life. OVERLEAF: the Homestead.

you can help out in the garden. For those wonderfully lazy moments that distinguish the perfect holiday, an age-worn wicker porch swing offers hours of total tranquility.

FLEMING JONES HOMESTEAD, 3170 Newtown Road, Placerville, CA 95667; (916) 626-5840; Janice Condit, Innkeeper. A historic 2-story farmhouse, built in 1883, with 3 guest rooms; 1 private bath, 2 shared, both have convenient wall grab bars. Rates: $40 to $55 double; single rates on request. Continental breakfast included. No children. No pets. No credit cards. A warm rural hospitality includes an invitation to explore 11 acres surrounding the farmhouse; feed the chickens; help in the garden; pet the animals; relax on the veranda and enjoy the Homestead rose garden with its many historic varieties of roses, some from early 1800s. In the area are found remnants of old gold mining sites; gold pans may be borrowed. Amador County wineries to be visited. Inn is open all year.

DIRECTIONS: On Rte. 50 pass through Placerville, take the Pt. View Drive exit to Broadway, turn left and continue on Broadway which runs parallel to hwy. and becomes Newtown Road. Continue on Newtown and watch for the "Homestead" sign. Up a driveway on the right sits the farmhouse.

This country guest room opens onto a second floor balcony.

Comfort and tradition in a boom-town hostelry

Formerly the ballroom, now an extravagantly furnished lobby.

The National, which first opened in 1854, is California's oldest continuously operating hotel. It occupies four adjoining brick buildings on Nevada City's Broad Street. Nothing in the hotel is just as it once was: an annex has come and gone; the present lobby—on the second floor—was once the ballroom. The bar was moved to its street-level location sometime in the 1920s and embellished with a lavish piece of woodwork from the Spreckels mansion in San Francisco. The previous innkeeper introduced the present color scheme that employs a liberal use of color, usually red. Tom Coleman, present innkeeper, agrees with the statement, "Its pretty hard to like the National if you don't like the color burgundy."

As the major hostelry of one of California's gold towns, the hotel has entertained generations of merchants, speculators, and visitors in high style. Many of its thirty guest rooms have curtained alcoves and wide, ornate Victorian bedsteads, and much of the furniture still has the stiff, store-bought opulence of a frontier town that has struck it rich. A few longtime guests use the lobby as their living room. It is both grand and homelike, with chandeliers, Victorian sofas, and oak armchairs. Hotel personnel bustle about, arranging a wedding reception, checking reservations for a couple coming in from Tokyo, or maybe just talking about the previous evening's meeting of the VFW Auxiliary.

French doors in the lobby open onto a terrace that provides a dramatic prospect of the quirky, charming town. Built on hills with random and precipitous streets, Nevada City still boasts many buildings from the boom days, including a beautiful theater—California's oldest—where Lola Montez, Oscar Wilde and Sarah Bernhardt appeared. Down the street, the American Victorian Museum houses a collection of artifacts from the area that reveals the exuberance of the young, thriving frontier.

Nevada City was cut out of the wilderness, and beyond the town are the forest and hills that once drew thousands of gold-hungry prospectors who came to make their fortune. Today, visitors and settlers can still reap a fortune in unpolluted air and Victorian charm.

Old-time, store-bought opulence.

NATIONAL HOTEL, 211 Broad St., Nevada City, CA 95959; (916) 265-4551; Thomas A. Coleman, Innkeeper. A 43-room hotel, with western-style saloon and Victorian dining room, in a former Sierra gold mining town. Private and shared baths. Open all year. Rates: $26 to $57 double. No breakfast served but there are several good restaurants nearby, including one at the American Victorian Museum that should not be missed. The hotel dining room, featuring an extensive and varied Continental menu, is highly recommended for lunch, dinner, and Sunday brunch. Children welcome. No pets. Visa, MasterCard accepted. Swimming pool, saloon, TV. Antiques and craft shops, historic buildings nearby.

DIRECTIONS: From Sacramento, take I-80 to Auburn, then Rte. 49 to Broad St. turnoff. Left on Broad St. across Deer Creek. Hotel is on the left.

Nevada City | # RED CASTLE INN | **GOLD COUNTRY**

A rare example of Gothic Revival

Deep in the hills of California's gold country is an exquisite example of Gothic Revival, a building style which combines the Victorian love of gingerbread with a Gothic look. The result is a superbly crafted building, in a style that we are only coming to appreciate today.

The Red Castle Inn, faithfully restored, looks hardly different than it did during the Gold Rush, when Judge John Williams built it as a home. Brickwork and fancy trim have been refurbished, and the interior has all of the original ceiling moldings and pine floors.

Jerry Ames and Chris Dickman, the new owners, have decorated the interior with Victorian furnishings and touches of Chinese, sensitively combined with latter-day, more comfortable furniture. A Story and Clark pump organ from the 1880s, commonly found in houses of that period, can be played by guests in the living room. There are wonderful wall hangings, and a collection of masks, displayed on the wall at the top of the staircase, is worth noticing.

One of the bedrooms opens onto the balcony overlooking Nevada City. Two are Victorian parlor suites, each with bedroom, sitting room, and bath. The innkeepers have left fresh-cut flowers and a decanter of sherry in every bedroom.

RED CASTLE INN, 109 Prospect, Nevada City, CA 95959; (916) 265-5135; Jerry Ames and Chris Dickman, Innkeepers. The colorful heyday of the Gold Rush is recalled in the decor of this 1860 red brick building. Set on a hill overlooking this historic town, the inn's terraced gardens, with a secluded pond, offer pleasant strolls. The inn has 7 guest rooms, 2 with parlors and private baths, and 3 bedrooms with private baths. The 2 rooms on the top floor share a parlor and a bath. Some rooms open onto balconies; the parlor has French doors leading onto the porch. The inn even has a legendary ghost, "Lady in Gray," who supposedly appears from time to time. Rates: $45 to $70, including Continental breakfast. No restaurant. Small children not encouraged. Pets accepted. Reservations recommended. Open all year. No credit cards accepted.

DIRECTIONS: From I-80, take Rte. 49 to Nevada City. Take Sacramento St. to Prospect.

The elegantly furnished living room.

A meticulous restoration devoted to authenticity

A fascinating history of the mid and late 1800s—encompassing the first discovery of gold, an early, prominent vineyard, extravagant entertaining, family tragedy, and ghosts in a town which, in its heyday, had a population of ten thousand, but which dropped to two hundred within a decade—is the setting for a popular inn and restaurant in Coloma.

Vineyard House is a seven-room inn with five dining areas and a saloon on the ground floor. Old kerosene lamps on each table light the 1870s furnishings. Pots of soup and salads are served in the same enamel bowls you can buy in the gift shop, located in one of the old parlors. Freshly baked bread accompanies the meal, of which chicken and dumplings is a favorite.

The meticulous restoration is being carried out by the innkeepers, Gary Herrera and his brother and sister-in-law, Frank and Darlene, and a friend, David Van Buskirk. They do it practically all themselves, from stripping floors and furniture to papering walls and making canopies and quilts.

Dedicated to authenticity, it is an all-consuming project that, now in its final stages of restoration, affords a delightful stay.

VINEYARD HOUSE, Cold Spring Road, P.O. Box 176, Coloma, CA 95613; (916) 622-2217; Frank, Darlene and Gary Herrera, David Van Buskirk, Innkeepers. The white Victorian house was built 105 years ago by Robert Chalmers as a hotel and home for his family. The inn is furnished with Victorian antiques, and the parlor has a cheerful fireplace. Dinner is served in 5 different areas, as well as on the porch in summer. The 7 guest rooms, all named after well-known Gold Rush personalities, share bath. Wash basins in all rooms. Rates: $35 to $50, Continental breakfast included. Restaurant and bar closed Mondays and Tuesdays, January to May. No children under 16. No pets. Open all year. Reservations required. Visa, MasterCard, American Express accepted. Historic attractions of Coloma include the park museum in the center of town and a working replica of John Sutter's sawmill where the first gold discovery was made in 1848.

DIRECTIONS: From US 50, turn north on Rte. 49 to Coloma, and Cold Spring Rd.

Where the original gold discovery was made.

PHOTOGRAPH BY JOHN M. DALY